# Dp ENGLISH STUDENT WORKBOOK

A Framework for Literary Analysis in IB Language A -
Literature/Language and Literature

**Damian Rentoule**

authorHOUSE®

*AuthorHouse™ UK Ltd.*
*500 Avebury Boulevard*
*Central Milton Keynes, MK9 2BE*
*www.authorhouse.co.uk*
*Phone: 08001974150*

*First published by AuthorHouse    03/26/2011*

*ISBN: 978-1-4567-7344-1*

*Any people depicted in stock imagery provided by Thinkstock are models,*
*and such images are being used for illustrative purposes only.*
*Certain stock imagery © Thinkstock.*

*This book is printed on acid-free paper.*

# CONTENTS

## Examples of Completed Activities

# Introduction

The exercises in this workbook are intended to develop the critical analytical skills that will help you to construct and articulate increasingly complex understandings of your texts. The structure is simple with eight flexible activities that are repeated for each text in the course.

Each activity has a space for you to write down your ideas about the connections that you are making between the different parts of the texts. There is a mix of individual and shared exercises as well as a mix of reading, writing, listening and speaking. As the activities are repeated for each text you will find that as you become more comfortable with the structure of the activities you will be able to return to earlier work and add ideas to your notes. The most important point is that constructing meaning and developing understanding takes time. Make sure that you give yourself time. Keep coming back to revise your earlier work. You will notice that there are two elements to a literary analysis: literary texts and their literary features.

You need to examine how these literary features work in each of your texts. The activities are introduced in the following format and all are intended to help you examine how the literary features are working in your texts.

## Activity: The name of the activity will appear here for ease of reference

**Assessment Criteria:** Here you will find an aspect of one of the assessment criteria.

**Description:** Here you will find a description of the activity. All activities have spaces to write answers and there are examples of completed activities at the back of this workbook so that you can see possible approaches.

All activities are based on a framework in which you need to fill in certain information and spaces are provided for this. This information will be valuable to look back on as you progress through the course and consolidate your understanding of your texts.

## *Text List*

To start please fill in the details of your texts for the next two years:

---

### **Your texts for this course**

---

*Text 1:* ...............................................................................

*Text 2:* ...............................................................................

*Text 3:* ...............................................................................

*Text 4:* ...............................................................................

*Text 5:* ...............................................................................

*Text 6:* ...............................................................................

*Text 7:* ...............................................................................

*Text 8:* ...............................................................................

*Text 9:* ...............................................................................

*Text 10:* ...............................................................................

*Text 11:* ...............................................................................

*Text 12:* ...............................................................................

*Text 13:* ...............................................................................

*Filling out the names of your texts on the contents page is also a good way to help you navigate the workbook.*

# The Framework

Many approaches to literary analysis are possible. The following diagram represents the approach that this Student Workbook will use to help you frame your literary responses to texts in a range of written and spoken tasks.

- From the numerous details in the text, literary features can be identified.

- These literary features support specific aspects of the text.

- These aspects of the text in turn support the ideas expressed in a text.

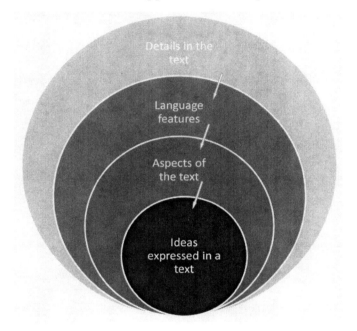

The purpose of this workbook is to examine the ways that we can use language to explain these connections in a clear, concise and precise manner. The activities presented in this workbook are designed to help you construct and articulate the connections between the parts of the texts that you are studying. When completing the activities please remember that a number of literary features always work together to support the ideas presented in a text. It would be a good idea to keep the following image in mind when working through the activities. For every idea presented you will be able to identify a large number of literary features that support the idea's presentation and your interpretation.

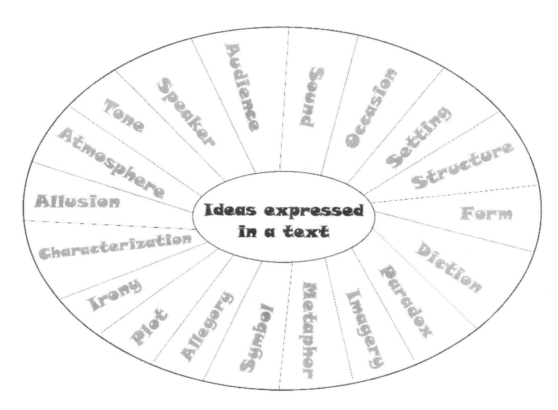

(Based on an idea of a 'Commentary Wheel' from an anonymous author presented at an IBAP Language A1 English Workshop in New Delhi, India February 2006)

# *Text One:*

**Assessment Criteria:** meaningful and perceptive linking of works / thorough knowledge and understanding of the content of the extract or works

**Description:** Before you start the course you already have a bank of knowledge that will help you to understand the texts. There may also be some misunderstandings that need clearing up.

- Write down notes regarding what you know about the text, author, time period, language or geographic region.

- In pairs share your own information and include new pieces of information from your partner in your workbook.

- During the course when you begin to look at a text as a class bring all your ideas together on the board to both share ideas and dispel misunderstandings.

## Text 1

**Title:**

**Author:**

**Dates:**

**Country and language of original publication:**

**What do you know about this text, author, time period, language, geographic region or political situation that may be relevant?**

## Activity 2: Quote Bank

**Assessment Criteria:** detailed and persuasive references to the works
**Description:**

- Choose a direct reference from a character in your text. In the case of poetry choose a specific line.

- Comment on the relevance of the reference – what it tells us about the character / poem.

- Finally, comment on the links between these references in terms of their significance for the text as a whole.

---
## Text:
---

**Character One:**

Quote / Reference 1:

Significance:

Quote / Reference 2:

Significance:

Quote / Reference 3:

Significance:

**Comment on the links between these quotes:**

---
## Text:
---

**Character Two:**

Quote / Reference 1:

Significance:

Quote / Reference 2:

Significance:

Quote / Reference 3:

Significance:

### Comment on the links between these quotes:

## Activity 3: Quote Builder

**Assessment Criteria:** ideas are convincing and show independence of thought
**Description:** Break into small groups or pairs. In turn each group or pair presents a short quote from the text to the opposing team.
The opposing team must supply three pieces of information after hearing the quote:

- Which character the quote is from
- The context in which it appeared in the text
- The significance of the quote for the overall text

The first two have definite answers although the last will be dependent on individual interpretations. All answers that can be justified are acceptable – the language used in the justification of the response is an important aspect of this activity.

## Quote Builder: Round 1 Notes

**Our Quote** (Write it here so you can read it out to the opposition)

**Character:**

**Context:**

**Significance:**

**Opposition Quote** (Just a few notes as you listen to it read out by the opposition)

**Character:**

**Context:**

**Significance:**

## Quote Builder: Round 2 Notes

**Our Quote** (Write it here so you can read it out to the opposition)

**Character:**

**Context:**

**Significance:**

**Opposition Quote** (Just a few notes as you listen to it read out by the opposition)

**Character:**

**Context:**

**Significance:**

## Activity 4: Literary Feature Analysis

**Assessment Criteria:** critical analysis of the effects of the literary features of the works consistently well illustrated by persuasive examples

**Description:**

- Copy a passage from your text into one of the spaces below.

- Identify a literary feature and comment on this feature in the 'Literary features' table.

Copy or paste a short passage from your text here

In this passage the author has made a range of choices regarding the way language is used. An author's style is formed through the patterns that these choices form. Just like in a physical landscape, ***physical features*** such as mountains and rivers stand out to the viewer – in literature, features of the language such as diction and imagery stand out to the reader or audience and these are ***literary features***.

## Literary Feature 1:

- Describe a literary feature that you can see in the passage above.

- Provide specific examples from the text.

- Describe the effect this literary feature has on the reader/audience.

- Outline links of this literary feature to others.

## Literary Feature 2:

- Describe a literary feature that you can see in the passage above.

- Provide specific examples from the text.

- Describe the effect this literary feature has on the reader/audience.

- Outline links of this literary feature to others.

---

## **Literary Feature 3:**

---

- Describe a literary feature that you can see in the passage above.

- Provide specific examples from the text.

- Describe the effect this literary feature has on the reader/audience.

- Outline links of this literary feature to others.

---

## **Literary Feature 4:**

---

- Describe a literary feature that you can see in the passage above.

- Provide specific examples from the text.

- Describe the effect this literary feature has on the reader/audience.

- Outline links of this literary feature to others.

## Activity 5: Shared Reading Response

**Assessment Criteria:** meaningful and perceptive linking of works
**Description:**

- In small groups students take turns speaking about the last thing that you read - generally the current work.
- The listener is required to ask questions as they go along using the following prompt.
- Both the listener and the speaker need to make note of any questions asked at the end of the activity

**Prompt to assist with questioning**

**As the listener you are required to ask questions related to any of the following:**

- **The speaker's knowledge of the content**

- **How parts of the work relate to the work as a whole and to other works?**

- **What effects literary features have on the reader's response?**

*As a listener you need to help the speaker stay focused and to support their ideas with specific references from the work. Your questioning can help them to do this. The speaker needs to use accurate, clear and precise language. By seeking clarification of points you can help the speaker to do this.*

**Shared Reading Response: Record Sheet for questions asked and responses**

## The speaker's knowledge of the content

## How parts of the work relate to the work as a whole and to other works?

## What effects literary features have on the reader's response?

## Other questions

## Activity 6: Connecting Theme and Literary Features in a Text

**Assessment Criteria:** in-depth knowledge of, and very good insight into, aspects of the work / purposeful and effective structure / supporting examples are well integrated

**Description:**

- Identify an idea, or theme, expressed through the text you are analyzing.

- Select up to three literary features that appear in the work that in some way support or are related to that identified idea or theme. Highlight these literary features from the given list. Definitions appear in the Vocabulary Log.

- Explain how the chosen literary features support this idea, or theme in the sections below.

- When completing the sections you should attempt to make links between the literary features in terms of how they support each other in the text.

---

## Text

---

**Theme/Ideas expressed through a text:**

**Literary features identified:**
Allegory, Alliteration, Allusion, Antagonist, Aside, Association, Assonance, Atmosphere, Audience, Blank Verse, Caesura, Caricature, Characterization, Climax, Connotation, Denotation, Denouement, Dialogue, Diction, Enjambment, Euphemism, Flashback, Foreshadowing, Form, Framed Narrative, Free Verse, Genre, Hyperbole, Imagery, Irony, Metaphor, Meter, Metonymy, Mood, Motif, Myth, Narrator, Occasion, Onomatopoeia, Paradox, Parody, Persona, Personification, Plot, Point of View, Protagonist, Repetition, Rhyme, Satire, Setting, Simile, Soliloquy, Sound, Speaker, Structure, Style, Subplot, Subtext, Symbol, Syntax (sentence structure), Theme, Tone

---

## Literary Feature 1

---

**Provide specific examples from the text.**

**Describe the effect this literary feature has on the reader/audience.**

**Outline links of this literary feature to other literary features.**

**Describe a literary feature that you can identify in your text.**

## Literary Feature 2

**Provide specific examples from the text.**

**Describe the effect this literary feature has on the reader/audience.**

**Outline links of this literary feature to other literary features.**

**Describe a literary feature that you can identify in your text.**

# Literary Feature 3

**Provide specific examples from the text.**

**Describe the effect this literary feature has on the reader/audience.**

**Outline links of this literary feature to other literary features.**

**Describe a literary feature that you can identify in your text.**

## Activity 7: Connecting Theme and Literary Features in a Text (Unseen)

**Assessment Criteria:** perceptive understanding of the thought and feeling expressed in the text as well as some of the subtleties of the text / detailed and persuasive references to the text / supporting examples are well integrated / in-depth knowledge of, and very good insight into, aspects of the work / purposeful and effective structure

**Description:** The instructions below are the same as for Activity 6 – you just need to repeat the process for this extract although you may not know the context within which this extract appears. The procedure is exactly the same.

- Identify an idea, or theme, expressed through the text.

- Select an important aspect of the text which supports this theme. Circle this word.

- Identify two literary features that support this aspect of the text. Circle these words.

- Explain how the chosen aspect of the text supports this theme.

- Explain how the chosen literary features support this aspect of the text.

- When you have completed these sections write it all out in one paragraph trying to make the connections as clear as possible.

### Sample extract 1: Albert Camus, *The Stranger*

It occurred to me that all I had to do was turn around and that would be the end of it.

But the whole beach, throbbing in the sun, was pressing on my back. I took a few steps toward the spring. The Arab didn't move. Besides, he was still pretty far away. Maybe it was the shadows on his face, but it looked like he was laughing. I waited. The sun was starting to burn my cheeks, and I could feel drops of sweat gathering in my eyebrows. The sun was the same as it had been the day I'd buried Maman, and like then, my forehead especially was hurting me, all the veins in it throbbing under the skin. It was this burning, which I couldn't stand anymore, that made me move forward.

I knew that it was stupid, that I wouldn't get the sun off me by stepping forward. But I took a step, one step, forward. And this time, without getting up, the Arab drew his knife and held it up to me in the sun. The light shot off the steel and it was like a long flashing blade cutting at my forehead. At the same instant the sweat in my eyebrows dripped down over my eyelids all at once and covered them with a warm, thick film. My eyes were blinded behind the curtain of tears and salt. All I could feel were the cymbals of sunlight crashing on my forehead and, indistinctly, the dazzling spear flying up from the knife in front of me. The scorching blade slashed at my eyelashes and stabbed at my stinging eyes. That's when everything began to reel. The sea carried up a thick, fiery breath. It seemed to me that the sky split open from one end to another to rain down fire. My whole being tensed and I squeezed my hand around the revolver. The trigger gave; I felt the smooth underside of the but; and there, in that noise, sharp and deafening at the same time, is where it all started. I shook off the sweat and sun. I knew that I had shattered the harmony of the day, the exceptional silence of the beach where I had been happy. Then I had

15

fired four more times at the motionless body where the bullets lodged without leaving a trace. And it was like knocking four quick times at the door of unhappiness.

(Camus, 1989; originally published in French in 1942)

---

## Text

---

**Theme/Ideas expressed through this extract:**

**Literary features identified:**

Allegory, Alliteration, Allusion, Antagonist, Aside, Association, Assonance, Atmosphere, Audience, Blank Verse, Caesura, Caricature, Characterization, Climax, Connotation, Denotation, Denouement, Dialogue, Diction, Enjambment, Euphemism, Flashback, Foreshadowing, Form, Framed Narrative, Free Verse, Genre, Hyperbole, Imagery, Irony, Metaphor, Meter, Metonymy, Mood, Motif, Myth, Narrator, Occasion, Onomatopoeia, Paradox, Parody, Persona, Personification, Plot, Point of View, Protagonist, Repetition, Rhyme, Satire, Setting, Simile, Soliloquy, Sound, Speaker, Structure, Style, Subplot, Subtext, Symbol, Syntax (sentence structure), Theme, Tone

## Literary Feature 1:

**Describe a literary feature in the extract.**

**Provide specific examples from the extract.**

**Describe the effect this literary feature has on the reader/audience.**

**Outline links of this literary feature to other literary features in the extract.**

## Literary Feature 2:

**Describe a literary feature in the extract.**

**Provide specific examples from the extract.**

**Describe the effect this literary feature has on the reader/audience.**

**Outline links of this literary feature to other literary features in the extract.**

---

## Literary Feature 3:

---

**Describe a literary feature in the extract.**

**Provide specific examples from the extract.**

**Describe the effect this literary feature has on the reader/audience.**

**Outline links of this literary feature to other literary features in the extract.**

## Activity 8: Analyzing Exam Questions

**Assessment Criteria:** Logical coherence; concise use of language; response to demands of question

**Description:**

- Choose an examination question from the following list. Identify works to which the question will be addressed.

- Identify and highlight the major concepts in the question. These are the words that you think are the most important; the essence of the question.

- Take these words and add some qualifying information showing how these words connect to the chosen works.

- Use these groups of words in your introductory paragraph.

- The words should also appear consistently throughout the rest of your response.

*Remember that exam questions present you with a wide range of possible aspects that you could use as ideas to pursue in other types of assignments such as oral commentaries. Over time this activity will provide you with a bank of ideas to use when analyzing literature.*

## Drama

"Comedy exposes human weakness; tragedy reveals human strength." How and to what extent does this claim apply to **at least two** of the plays you have studied?

A change in status of the characters in a play (a success, for example, a loss or exposure) helps to convey the ideas and/or values of the dramatist. How and to what extent has change in status contributed in this way to **at least two** of the plays you have studied?

## Poetry

To what extent does the sense of hearing a voice or voices intensify the impact of a poem? Consider this question with close reference to works by **at least two** of the poets in your study.

## Prose: The Novel and Short Story

"The past is forever in the present." How does the use of narrative techniques, in **at least two** of the works you have studied, demonstrate whether or not this statement is valid?

## Prose: Other than the Novel or Short Story

"Daily life is the stuff of which high sanctity can be made." Discuss how far and in what ways **at least two** of the prose works you have studied have treated daily life in such a way as to raise it above the "everyday".

## General Questions on Literature

Some writers make us see people's lives through the lens of nostalgia. In what ways have writers used nostalgia in **at least two** of the works you have studied?

Images of sickness, both real and metaphorical, can reflect corruption in individuals and/or society. To what degree and to what effect is this evident in **at least two** of the works you have studied?

(IB May Paper 2 2008 TZ2)

**Highlight the question that you have selected from the list above. In the space below write the words that you have chosen from that question; the essence of the question.**

**Write down your thoughts regarding how these words relate to the work/s that you will be addressing.**

**Based on these thoughts add some qualifying information to the words to show how they connect to the chosen works.**

**Write an introductory paragraph with these words appearing multiple times. Remember that you chose them because they were the essence of the question.**

# *Text Two:*

**Assessment Criteria:** meaningful and perceptive linking of works / thorough knowledge and understanding of the content of the extract or works

**Description:** Before you start the course you already have a bank of knowledge that will help you to understand the texts. There may also be some misunderstandings that need clearing up.

- Write down notes regarding what you know about the text, author, time period, language or geographic region.
- In pairs share your own information and include new pieces of information from your partner in your workbook.
- During the course when you begin to look at a text as a class bring all your ideas together on the board to both share ideas and dispel misunderstandings.

## Text 2

**Title:**

**Author:**

**Dates:**

**Country and language of original publication:**

**What do you know about this text, author, time period, language, geographic region or political situation that may be relevant?**

# Activity 2: Quote Bank

**Assessment Criteria:** detailed and persuasive references to the works
**Description:**

- Choose a direct reference from a character in your text. In the case of poetry choose a specific line.

- Comment on the relevance of the reference – what it tells us about the character / poem.

- Finally, comment on the links between these references in terms of their significance for the text as a whole.

---

## Text:

---

**Character One:**


Quote / Reference 1:


Significance:


Quote / Reference 2:


Significance:


Quote / Reference 3:


Significance:


**Comment on the links between these quotes:**

## Text:

**Character Two:**

Quote / Reference 1:

Significance:

Quote / Reference 2:

Significance:

Quote / Reference 3:

Significance:

**Comment on the links between these quotes:**

## Activity 3: Quote Builder

**Assessment Criteria:** ideas are convincing and show independence of thought

**Description:** Break into small groups or pairs. In turn each group or pair presents a short quote from the text to the opposing team.

The opposing team must supply three pieces of information after hearing the quote:

- Which character the quote is from
- The context in which it appeared in the text
- The significance of the quote for the overall text

The first two have definite answers although the last will be dependent on individual interpretations. All answers that can be justified are acceptable – the language used in the justification of the response is an important aspect of this activity.

## Quote Builder: Round 1 Notes

**Our Quote** (Write it here so you can read it out to the opposition)


**Character:**


**Context:**


**Significance:**


**Opposition Quote** (Just a few notes as you listen to it read out by the opposition)


**Character:**


**Context:**


**Significance:**

# Quote Builder: Round 2 Notes

**Our Quote** (Write it here so you can read it out to the opposition)

**Character:**

**Context:**

**Significance:**

**Opposition Quote** (Just a few notes as you listen to it read out by the opposition)

**Character:**

**Context:**

**Significance:**

## Activity 3: Literary Feature Analysis

**Assessment Criteria:** critical analysis of the effects of the literary features of the works consistently well illustrated by persuasive examples

**Description:**

- Copy a passage from your text into one of the spaces below.
- Identify a literary feature and comment on this feature in the 'Literary features' table.

Copy or paste a short passage from your text here

## Literary Feature 1:

- Describe a literary feature that you can see in the passage above.

- Provide specific examples from the text.

- Describe the effect this literary feature has on the reader/audience.

- Outline links of this literary feature to others.

## Literary Feature 2:

- Describe a literary feature that you can see in the passage above.

- Provide specific examples from the text.

- Describe the effect this literary feature has on the reader/audience.

- Outline links of this literary feature to others.

---

## Literary Feature 3:

---

- Describe a literary feature that you can see in the passage above.

- Provide specific examples from the text.

- Describe the effect this literary feature has on the reader/audience.

- Outline links of this literary feature to others.

---

## Literary Feature 4:

---

- Describe a literary feature that you can see in the passage above.

- Provide specific examples from the text.

- Describe the effect this literary feature has on the reader/audience.

- Outline links of this literary feature to others.

## Activity 4: Shared Reading Response

**Assessment Criteria:** meaningful and perceptive linking of works
**Description:**

- In small groups students take turns speaking about the last thing that you read - generally the current work.
- The listener is required to ask questions as they go along using the following prompt.
- Both the listener and the speaker need to make note of any questions asked at the end of the activity

**Prompt to assist with questioning**

**As the listener you are required to ask questions related to any of the following:**

- **The speaker's knowledge of the content**

- **How parts of the work relate to the work as a whole and to other works?**

- **What effects literary features have on the reader's response?**

As a listener you need to help the speaker stay focused and to support their ideas with specific references from the work. Your questioning can help them to do this. The speaker needs to use accurate, clear and precise language. By seeking clarification of points you can help the speaker to do this.

**Shared Reading Response: Record Sheet for questions asked and responses**

## The speaker's knowledge of the content

## How parts of the work relate to the work as a whole and to other works?

## What effects literary features have on the reader's response?

## Other questions

## Activity 5: Connecting Theme and Literary Features in a Text

**Assessment Criteria:** in-depth knowledge of, and very good insight into, aspects of the work / purposeful and effective structure / supporting examples are well integrated
**Description:**

- Identify an idea, or theme, expressed through the text you are analyzing.

- Select up to three literary features that appear in the work that in some way support or are related to that identified idea or theme. Highlight these literary features from the given list. Definitions appear in the Vocabulary Log.

- Explain how the chosen literary features support this idea, or theme in the sections below.

- When completing the sections you should attempt to make links between the literary features in terms of how they support each other in the text.

---

# Text:

---

**Theme/Ideas expressed through a text:**

**Literary features identified:**
Allegory, Alliteration, Allusion, Antagonist, Aside, Association, Assonance, Atmosphere, Audience, Blank Verse, Caesura, Caricature, Characterization, Climax, Connotation, Denotation, Denouement, Dialogue, Diction, Enjambment, Euphemism, Flashback, Foreshadowing, Form, Framed Narrative, Free Verse, Genre, Hyperbole, Imagery, Irony, Metaphor, Meter, Metonymy, Mood, Motif, Myth, Narrator, Occasion, Onomatopoeia, Paradox, Parody, Persona, Personification, Plot, Point of View, Protagonist, Repetition, Rhyme, Satire, Setting, Simile, Soliloquy, Sound, Speaker, Structure, Style, Subplot, Subtext, Symbol, Syntax (sentence structure), Theme, Tone

---

## Literary Feature 1:

**Describe a literary feature that you can identify in your text.**

**Provide specific examples from the text.**

**Describe the effect this literary feature has on the reader/audience.**

**Outline links of this literary feature to other literary features.**

## Literary Feature 2:

**Describe a literary feature that you can identify in your text.**

**Provide specific examples from the text.**

**Describe the effect this literary feature has on the reader/audience.**

**Outline links of this literary feature to other literary features.**

## Literary Feature 3:

**Describe a literary feature that you can identify in your text.**

**Provide specific examples from the text.**

**Describe the effect this literary feature has on the reader/audience.**

**Outline links of this literary feature to other literary features.**

## Activity 6: Connecting Theme and Literary Features in a Text (Unseen)

**Assessment Criteria:** perceptive understanding of the thought and feeling expressed in the text as well as some of the subtleties of the text / detailed and persuasive references to the text / supporting examples are well integrated / in-depth knowledge of, and very good insight into, aspects of the work / purposeful and effective structure

**Description:** The instructions below are the same as for Activity 6 – you just need to repeat the process for this extract although you may not know the context within which this extract appears. The procedure is exactly the same.

- Identify an idea, or theme, expressed through the text.

- Select an important aspect of the text which supports this theme. Circle this word.

- Identify two literary features that support this aspect of the text. Circle these words.

- Explain how the chosen aspect of the text supports this theme.

- Explain how the chosen literary features support this aspect of the text.

- When you have completed these sections write it all out in one paragraph trying to make the connections as clear as possible.

### Sample extract 2: Gabriel García Márquez, 'I only came to use the phone' from *Strange Pilgrims*

One rainy spring afternoon, while Maria de la Luz Cervantes was driving alone back to Barcelona, her rented car broke down in the Monegros desert. She was twenty-seven years old, a thoughtful, pretty Mexican who had enjoyed a certain fame as a music hall performer a few years earlier. She was married to a cabaret magician, whom she was to meet later that day after visiting some relatives in Zaragoza. For an hour she made desperate signals to the cars and trucks that sped past her in the storm, until at last the driver of a ramshackle bus took pity on her. He did warn her, however, that he was not going very far.

"It does not matter," said Maria. "All I need is a telephone."

That was true, and she needed it only to let her husband know that she would not be home be home before seven. Wearing a student's coat and beach shoes in April, she looked like a bedraggled bird, and she was so distraught after her mishap that she forgot to take the car keys. A women with a military air was sitting next to the driver, and she gave Maria a towel and a blanket and made some room for her on the seat. Maria wiped off the worst of the rain and then sat down, wrapped herself in the blanket, and tried to light a cigarette, but her matches were wet. The woman sharing the seat gave her a light and asked for one of the few cigarettes that were still dry. While they smoked, Maria gave in to a desire to vent her feelings and raised her voice over the noise of the rain and the clatter of the bus. The woman interrupted her by placing a ner lips.

asleep,' she whispered.

Maria looked over her shoulder and saw that the bus was full of women of uncertain ages and varying conditions who were sleeping in blankets just like hers. Their serenity was contagious, and Maria curled up in her seat and succumbed to the sound of the rain. When she awoke, it was dark and the storm had dissolved into an icy drizzle. She had no idea how long she had slept or in what place in the world they had come to. Her neighbor looked watchful.

'Where are we?' Maria asked.

'We've arrived,' answered the woman.

The bus was entering the cobbled courtyard of an enormous, gloomy building that seemed to be an old convent in a forest of colossal trees. The passengers, just visible in the dim light of a lamp in the courtyard, sat motionless until the woman with the military air ordered them out of the bus with the kind of primitive directions used in nursery school. They were all older woman, and their movements.......

(Marquez, 1994; originally published in Spanish in 1992)

---

## Text:

---

**Theme/Ideas expressed through this extract:**

**Literary features identified:**
Allegory, Alliteration, Allusion, Antagonist, Aside, Association, Assonance, Atmosphere, Audience, Blank Verse, Caesura, Caricature, Characterization, Climax, Connotation, Denotation, Denouement, Dialogue, Diction, Enjambment, Euphemism, Flashback, Foreshadowing, Form, Framed Narrative, Free Verse, Genre, Hyperbole, Imagery, Irony, Metaphor, Meter, Metonymy, Mood, Motif, Myth, Narrator, Occasion, Onomatopoeia, Paradox, Parody, Persona, Personification, Plot, Point of View, Protagonist, Repetition, Rhyme, Satire, Setting, Simile, Soliloquy, Sound, Speaker, Structure, Style, Subplot, Subtext, Symbol, Syntax (sentence structure), Theme, Tone

---

## Literary Feature 1:

---

**Describe a literary feature in the extract.**

**Provide specific examples from the extract.**

**Describe the effect this literary feature has on the reader/audience.**

**Outline links of this literary feature to other literary features in the extract.**

## Literary Feature 2:

**Describe a literary feature in the extract.**

**Provide specific examples from the extract.**

**Describe the effect this literary feature has on the reader/audience.**

**Outline links of this literary feature to other literary features in the extract**

## Literary Feature 3:

**Describe a literary feature in the extract.**

**Provide specific examples from the extract.**

**Describe the effect this literary feature has on the reader/audience.**

**Outline links of this literary feature to other literary features in the extract.**

**Assessment Criteria:** Logical coherence; concise use of language; response to demands of question
**Description:**

- Choose an examination question from the following list. Identify works to which the question will be addressed.

- Identify and highlight the major concepts in the question. These are the words that you think are the most important; the essence of the question.

- Take these words and add some qualifying information showing how these words connect to the chosen works.

- Use these groups of words in your introductory paragraph.

- The words should also appear consistently throughout the rest of your response.

*Remember that exam questions present you with a wide range of possible aspects that you could use as ideas to pursue in other types of assignments such as oral commentaries. Over time this activity will provide you with a bank of ideas to use when analyzing literature.*

## Drama

A change in status of the characters in a play (a success, for example, a loss or exposure) helps to convey the ideas and/or values of the dramatist. How and to what extent has change in status contributed in this way to **at least two** of the plays you have studied?

## Poetry

Pattern is an important element in poetry. What patterns can be discerned in the poems you have studied? Identify these and discuss how and to what effect they are used in poems by **at least two** poets you have studied.

## Prose: The Novel and Short Story

Justify, with close reference to **at least two** of the texts you have studied, your judgments as to whether their endings are fitting in the light of what has gone before.

## Prose: Other than the Novel or Short Story

Prose other than the novel or short story often expresses strong political and/or ethical views. To what extent is this true of **at least two** of the works you have studied, and in what ways and to what extent have the writers made such views convincing?

## General Questions on Literature

Urban settings are often portrayed as "spiritual wastelands". To what extent, if at all, and by what means, have **at least two** of the works you have studied presented urban settings in such a way?

"All Art is quite useless." With close reference to **at least two** of the texts you have studied discuss and give reasons for the extent to which you agree or disagree with this statement.

(IB May Paper 2 2008 TZ2)

**Highlight the question that you have selected from the list above. In the space below write the words that you have chosen from that question; the essence of the question.**

**Write down your thoughts regarding how these words relate to the work/s that you will be addressing.**

**Based on these thoughts add some qualifying information to the words to show how they connect to the chosen works.**

**Write an introductory paragraph with these words appearing multiple times. Remember that you chose them because they were the essence of the question.**

## *Text Three:*

**Assessment Criteria:** meaningful and perceptive linking of works / thorough knowledge and understanding of the content of the extract or works

**Description:** Before you start the course you already have a bank of knowledge that will help you to understand the texts. There may also be some misunderstandings that need clearing up.

- Write down notes regarding what you know about the text, author, time period, language or geographic region.

- In pairs share your own information and include new pieces of information from your partner in your workbook.

- During the course when you begin to look at a text as a class bring all your ideas together on the board to both share ideas and dispel misunderstandings.

## Text 3

**Title:**

**Author:**

**Dates:**

**Country and language of original publication:**

**What do you know about this text, author, time period, language, geographic region or political situation that may be relevant?**

## Activity 2: Quote Bank

**Assessment Criteria:** detailed and persuasive references to the works
**Description:**

- Choose a direct reference from a character in your text. In the case of poetry choose a specific line.

- Comment on the relevance of the reference – what it tells us about the character / poem.

- Finally, comment on the links between these references in terms of their significance for the text as a whole.

---

## Text:

---

**Character One:**

Quote / Reference 1:

Significance:

Quote / Reference 2:

Significance:

Quote / Reference 3:

Significance:

**Comment on the links between these quotes:**

---

## Text:

---

**Character Two:**

Quote / Reference 1:

Significance:

Quote / Reference 2:

Significance:

Quote / Reference 3:

Significance:

**Comment on the links between these quotes:**

## Activity 3: Quote Builder

**Assessment Criteria:** ideas are convincing and show independence of thought
**Description:** Break into small groups or pairs. In turn each group or pair presents a short quote from the text to the opposing team.
The opposing team must supply three pieces of information after hearing the quote:

- Which character the quote is from
- The context in which it appeared in the text
- The significance of the quote for the overall text

The first two have definite answers although the last will be dependent on individual interpretations. All answers that can be justified are acceptable – the language used in the justification of the response is an important aspect of this activity.

## Quote Builder: Round 1 Notes

**Our Quote** (Write it here so you can read it out to the opposition)

**Character:**

**Context:**

**Significance:**

**Opposition Quote** (Just a few notes as you listen to it read out by the opposition)

**Character:**

**Context:**

**Significance:**

# Quote Builder: Round 2 Notes

**Our Quote** (Write it here so you can read it out to the opposition)

**Character:**

**Context:**

**Significance:**

**Opposition Quote** (Just a few notes as you listen to it read out by the opposition)

**Character:**

**Context:**

**Significance:**

## Activity 4: Literary Feature Analysis

**Assessment Criteria:** critical analysis of the effects of the literary features of the works consistently well illustrated by persuasive examples

**Description:**

- Copy a passage from your text into one of the spaces below.
- Identify a literary feature and comment on this feature in the 'Literary features' table.

Copy or paste a short passage from your text here

## Literary Feature 1:

- Describe a literary feature that you can see in the passage above.


- Provide specific examples from the text.


- Describe the effect this literary feature has on the reader/audience.


- Outline links of this literary feature to others.


## Literary Feature 2:

- Describe a literary feature that you can see in the passage above.


- Provide specific examples from the text.


- Describe the effect this literary feature has on the reader/audience.


- Outline links of this literary feature to others.

## Literary Feature 3:

- Describe a literary feature that you can see in the passage above.

- Provide specific examples from the text.

- Describe the effect this literary feature has on the reader/audience.

- Outline links of this literary feature to others.

## Literary Feature 4:

- Describe a literary feature that you can see in the passage above.

- Provide specific examples from the text.

- Describe the effect this literary feature has on the reader/audience.

- Outline links of this literary feature to others.

# Activity 5: Shared Reading Response

**Assessment Criteria:** meaningful and perceptive linking of works
**Description:**

- In small groups students take turns speaking about the last thing that you read - generally the current work.
- The listener is required to ask questions as they go along using the following prompt.
- Both the listener and the speaker need to make note of any questions asked at the end of the activity

**Prompt to assist with questioning**

**As the listener you are required to ask questions related to any of the following:**

- **The speaker's knowledge of the content**

- **How parts of the work relate to the work as a whole and to other works?**

- **What effects literary features have on the reader's response?**

*As a listener you need to help the speaker stay focused and to support their ideas with specific references from the work. Your questioning can help them to do this. The speaker needs to use accurate, clear and precise language. By seeking clarification of points you can help the speaker to do this.*

**Shared Reading Response: Record Sheet for questions asked and responses**

## The speaker's knowledge of the content

## How parts of the work relate to the work as a whole and to other works?

## What effects literary features have on the reader's response?

## Other questions

## Activity 6: Connecting Theme and Literary Features in a Text

**Assessment Criteria:** in-depth knowledge of, and very good insight into, aspects of the work / purposeful and effective structure / supporting examples are well integrated

**Description:**

- Identify an idea, or theme, expressed through the text you are analyzing.

- Select up to three literary features that appear in the work that in some way support or are related to that identified idea or theme. Highlight these literary features from the given list. Definitions appear in the Vocabulary Log.

- Explain how the chosen literary features support this idea, or theme in the sections below.

- When completing the sections you should attempt to make links between the literary features in terms of how they support each other in the text.

---

# Text:

---

**Theme/Ideas expressed through a text:**

**Literary features identified:**

Allegory, Alliteration, Allusion, Antagonist, Aside, Association, Assonance, Atmosphere, Audience, Blank Verse, Caesura, Caricature, Characterization, Climax, Connotation, Denotation, Denouement, Dialogue, Diction, Enjambment, Euphemism, Flashback, Foreshadowing, Form, Framed Narrative, Free Verse, Genre, Hyperbole, Imagery, Irony, Metaphor, Meter, Metonymy, Mood, Motif, Myth, Narrator, Occasion, Onomatopoeia, Paradox, Parody, Persona, Personification, Plot, Point of View, Protagonist, Repetition, Rhyme, Satire, Setting, Simile, Soliloquy, Sound, Speaker, Structure, Style, Subplot, Subtext, Symbol, Syntax (sentence structure), Theme, Tone

## Literary Feature 1:

**Provide specific examples from the text**

**Describe the effect this literary feature has on the reader/audience.**

**Outline links of this literary feature to other literary features in the extract.**

## Literary Feature 3:

**Provide specific examples from the text.**

**Describe the effect this literary feature has on the reader/audience.**

**Outline links of this literary feature to other literary features.Literary Feature**

## Activity 7: Connecting Theme and Literary Features in a Text (Unseen)

**Assessment Criteria:** perceptive understanding of the thought and feeling expressed in the text as well as some of the subtleties of the text / detailed and persuasive references to the text / supporting examples are well integrated / in-depth knowledge of, and very good insight into, aspects of the work / purposeful and effective structure

**Description:** The instructions below are the same as for Activity 6 – you just need to repeat the process for this extract although you may not know the context within which this extract appears. The procedure is exactly the same.

- Identify an idea, or theme, expressed through the text.

- Select an important aspect of the text which supports this theme. Circle this word.

- Identify two literary features that support this aspect of the text. Circle these words.

- Explain how the chosen aspect of the text supports this theme.

- Explain how the chosen literary features support this aspect of the text.

- When you have completed these sections write it all out in one paragraph trying to make the connections as clear as possible.

### Sample extract 3: Anton Chekhov, *The Seagull*

## ACT 1

The scene is laid in the park on SORIN'S estate. A broad avenue of trees leads away from the audience toward a lake which lies lost in the depths of the park. The avenue is obstructed by a rough stage, temporarily erected for the performance of amateur theatricals, and which screens the lake from view. There is a dense growth of bushes to the left and right of the stage. A few chairs and a little table are placed in front of the stage. The sun has just set. JACOB and some other workmen are heard hammering and coughing on the stage behind the lowered curtain.

MASHA and MEDVIEDENKO come in from the left, returning from a walk.

MEDVIEDENKO
Why do you always wear mourning?

MASHA
I dress in black to match my life. I am unhappy.

## MEDVIEDENKO

Why should you be unhappy? [Thinking it over] I don't understand it. You are healthy, and though your father is not rich, he has a good competency. My life is far harder than yours. I only have twenty-three roubles a month to live on, but I don't wear mourning. [They sit down].

## MASHA

Happiness does not depend on riches; poor men are often happy.

## MEDVIEDENKO

In theory, yes, but not in reality. Take my case, for instance; my mother, my two sisters, my little brother and I must all live somehow on my salary of twenty-three roubles a month. We have to eat and drink, I take it. You wouldn't have us go without tea and sugar, would you? Or tobacco? Answer me that, if you can.

## MASHA

[Looking in the direction of the stage] The play will soon begin.

## MEDVIEDENKO

Yes, Nina Zarietchnaya is going to act in Treplieff's play. They love one another, and their two souls will unite to-night in the effort to interpret the same idea by different means. There is no ground on which your soul and mine can meet. I love you. Too restless and sad to stay at home, I tramp here every day, six miles and back, to be met only by your indifference. I am poor, my family is large, you can have no inducement to marry a man who cannot even find sufficient food for his own mouth.

## MASHA

It is not that. [She takes snuff] I am touched by your affection, but I cannot return it, that is all. [She offers him the snuff-box] Will you take some?

## MEDVIEDENKO

No, thank you. [A pause.]

## MASHA

The air is sultry; a storm is brewing for to-night. You do nothing but moralise or else talk about money. To you, poverty is the greatest misfortune that can befall a man, but I think it is a thousand times easier to go begging in rags than to-- You wouldn't understand that, though.

SORIN leaning on a cane, and TREPLIEFF come in.

## SORIN

For some reason, my boy, country life doesn't suit me, and I am sure I shall never get used to it. Last night I went to bed at ten and woke at nine this morning, feeling as if, from oversleep, my brain had stuck to my skull. [Laughing] And yet I accidentally dropped off to sleep again after dinner, and feel utterly done up at this moment. It is like a nightmare.

## TREPLIEFF

There is no doubt that you should live in town. [He catches sight of MASHA and MEDVIEDENKO] You shall be called when the play begins, my friends, but you must not stay here now. Go away, please.

## SORIN

Miss Masha, will you kindly ask your father to leave the dog unchained? It howled so last night that my sister was unable to sleep.

## MASHA

You must speak to my father yourself. Please excuse me; I can't do so. [To MEDVIEDENKO] Come, let us go.

## MEDVIEDENKO

You will let us know when the play begins?

MASHA and MEDVIEDENKO go out.

## SORIN

I foresee that that dog is going to howl all night again. It is always this way in the country; I have never been able to live as I like here. I come down for a month's holiday, to rest and all, and am plagued so by their nonsense that I long to escape after the first day. [Laughing] I have always been glad to get away from this place, but I have been retired now, and this was the only place I had to come to. Willy-nilly, one must live somewhere.

## JACOB

[To TREPLIEFF] We are going to take a swim, Mr. Constantine.

## TREPLIEFF

Very well, but you must be back in ten minutes.

## JACOB

We will, sir.

## TREPLIEFF

[Looking at the stage] Just like a real theatre! See, there we have the curtain, the foreground, the background, and all. No artificial scenery is needed. The eye travels direct to the lake, and rests on the horizon. The curtain will be raised as the moon rises at half-past eight.

## SORIN

Splendid!

## TREPLIEFF

Of course the whole effect will be ruined if Nina is late. She should be here by now, but her father and stepmother watch her so closely that it is like stealing her from a prison to get her away from home. [He straightens SORIN'S collar] Your hair and beard are all on end. Oughtn't you to have them trimmed?

## SORIN

[Smoothing his beard] They are the tragedy of my existence. Even when I was young I always looked as if I were drunk, and all. Women have never liked me. [Sitting down] Why is my sister out of temper?

## TREPLIEFF

Why? Because she is jealous and bored. [Sitting down beside SORIN] She is not acting this evening, but Nina is, and so she has set herself against me, and against the performance of the play, and against the play itself, which she hates without ever having read it.

## SORIN

[Laughing] Does she, really?

(Chekhov, 1990; originally published in Russian in 1901)

---

## Text:

---

**Theme/Ideas expressed through this extract:**


**Literary features identified:**

Allegory, Alliteration, Allusion, Antagonist, Aside, Association, Assonance, Atmosphere, Audience, Blank Verse, Caesura, Caricature, Characterization, Climax, Connotation, Denotation, Denouement, Dialogue, Diction, Enjambment, Euphemism, Flashback, Foreshadowing, Form, Framed Narrative, Free Verse, Genre, Hyperbole, Imagery, Irony, Metaphor, Meter, Metonymy, Mood, Motif, Myth, Narrator, Occasion, Onomatopoeia, Paradox, Parody, Persona, Personification, Plot, Point of View, Protagonist, Repetition, Rhyme, Satire, Setting, Simile, Soliloquy, Sound, Speaker, Structure, Style, Subplot, Subtext, Symbol, Syntax (sentence structure), Theme, Tone

## Literary Feature 1:

**Describe a literary feature in the extract.**

**Provide specific examples from the extract.**

**Describe the effect this literary feature has on the reader/audience.**

**Outline links of this literary feature to other literary features in the extract.**

## Literary Feature 2:

**Describe a literary feature in the extract.**

**Provide specific examples from the extract.**

**Describe the effect this literary feature has on the reader/audience.**

**Outline links of this literary feature to other literary features in the extract.**

## Literary Feature 3:

**Describe a literary feature in the extract.**

**Provide specific examples from the extract.**

**Describe the effect this literary feature has on the reader/audience.**

**Outline links of this literary feature to other literary features in the extract.**

## Activity 8: Analyzing Exam Questions

**Assessment Criteria:** Logical coherence; concise use of language; response to demands of question
**Description:**

- Choose an examination question from the following list. Identify works to which the question will be addressed.

- Identify and highlight the major concepts in the question. These are the words that you think are the most important; the essence of the question.

- Take these words and add some qualifying information showing how these words connect to the chosen works.

- Use these groups of words in your introductory paragraph.

- The words should also appear consistently throughout the rest of your response.

*Remember that exam questions present you with a wide range of possible aspects that you could use as ideas to pursue in other types of assignments such as oral commentaries. Over time this activity will provide you with a bank of ideas to use when analyzing literature.*

## Drama

"What is drama but life with the dull bits cut out?" To what extent do you find this statement applicable in **at least two** plays you have studied?

## Poetry

Some poets look from the particular to the universal to explore human experience. Discuss poems from **at least two** poets in relation to this statement, considering also the ways in which they achieve their effects.

## Prose: The Novel and Short Story

Discuss the ways in which **at least two** novels or short stories you have studied demonstrate that the search for identity can be a conscious or an unconscious process.

## Prose: Other than the Novel or Short Story

A writer usually attempts to create a bond of trust between writer and reader. How and to what extent have **at least two** writers you have studied been able to elicit your trust?

## General Questions on Literature

"Why won't writers allow children simply to be children?" Discuss the presentation and significance of children, or the state of childhood, in **at least two** works you have studied in the light of this complaint.

"Art is a lie that makes us realize the truth." Discuss **at least two** works you have studied in light of this statement, and say how far you would agree with it.

(IB, Paper 2, May 2008 TZ1)

**Highlight the question that you have selected from the list above. In the space below write the words that you have chosen from that question; the essence of the question.**

**Write down your thoughts regarding how these words relate to the work/s that you will be addressing.**

**Based on these thoughts add some qualifying information to the words to show how they connect to the chosen works.**

**Write an introductory paragraph with these words appearing multiple times. Remember that you chose them because they were the essence of the question.**

# *Text Four:*

*Some Advice: When you are speaking or writing about a text, try to use as many quotes as possible. They don't have to be long or word for word for that matter as you can paraphrase. For example, when in Shakespeare's Othello Iago speaks of the 'monstrous birth' of his plan,' You don't have to remember the exact words. In this case just those two words that you recall are enough. This use of direct references will demonstrate clearly your knowledge of the text.*

## Activity 1: Considering Context

**Assessment Criteria:** meaningful and perceptive linking of works / thorough knowledge and understanding of the content of the extract or works

**Description:** Before you start the course you already have a bank of knowledge that will help you to understand the texts. There may also be some misunderstandings that need clearing up.

- Write down notes regarding what you know about the text, author, time period, language or geographic region.

- In pairs share your own information and include new pieces of information from your partner in your workbook.

- During the course when you begin to look at a text as a class bring all your ideas together on the board to both share ideas and dispel misunderstandings.

---

## Text 4

---

**Title:**


**Author:**


**Dates:**


**Country and language of original publication:**


**What do you know about this text, author, time period, language, geographic region or political situation that may be relevant?**

## Activity 2: Quote Bank

**Assessment Criteria:** detailed and persuasive references to the works
**Description:**

- Choose a direct reference from a character in your text. In the case of poetry choose a specific line.
- Comment on the relevance of the reference – what it tells us about the character / poem.
- Finally, comment on the links between these references in terms of their significance for the text as a whole.

---

# Text:

---

**Character One:**

Quote / Reference 1:

Significance:

Quote / Reference 2:

Significance:

Quote / Reference 3:

Significance:

**Comment on the links between these quotes:**

---

## Text:

---

**Character Two:**

Quote / Reference 1:

Significance:

Quote / Reference 2:

Significance:

Quote / Reference 3:

Significance:

**Comment on the links between these quotes:**

## Activity 3: Quote Builder

**Assessment Criteria:** ideas are convincing and show independence of thought
**Description:** Break into small groups or pairs. In turn each group or pair presents a short quote from the text to the opposing team.
The opposing team must supply three pieces of information after hearing the quote:

- Which character the quote is from
- The context in which it appeared in the text
- The significance of the quote for the overall text

The first two have definite answers although the last will be dependent on individual interpretations. All answers that can be justified are acceptable – the language used in the justification of the response is an important aspect of this activity.

## Quote Builder: Round 1 Notes

**Our Quote** (Write it here so you can read it out to the opposition)

**Character:**

**Context:**

**Significance:**

**Opposition Quote** (Just a few notes as you listen to it read out by the opposition)

**Character:**

**Context:**

**Significance:**

## Quote Builder: Round 2 Notes

**Our Quote** (Write it here so you can read it out to the opposition)

**Character:**

**Context:**

**Significance:**

**Opposition Quote** (Just a few notes as you listen to it read out by the opposition)

**Character:**

**Context:**

**Significance:**

## Activity 4: Literary Feature Analysis

**Assessment Criteria:** critical analysis of the effects of the literary features of the works consistently well illustrated by persuasive examples

**Description:**

- Copy a passage from your text into one of the spaces below.

- Identify a literary feature and comment on this feature in the 'Literary features' table.

---

### Copy or paste a short passage from your text here

---

## Literary Feature 1:

- Describe a literary feature that you can see in the passage above.

- Provide specific examples from the text.

- Describe the effect this literary feature has on the reader/audience.

- Outline links of this literary feature to others.

## Literary Feature 2:

- Describe a literary feature that you can see in the passage above.

- Provide specific examples from the text.

- Describe the effect this literary feature has on the reader/audience.

- Outline links of this literary feature to others.

## Literary Feature 3:

- Describe a literary feature that you can see in the passage above.

- Provide specific examples from the text.

- Describe the effect this literary feature has on the reader/audience.

- Outline links of this literary feature to others.

## Literary Feature 4:

- Describe a literary feature that you can see in the passage above.

- Provide specific examples from the text.

- Describe the effect this literary feature has on the reader/audience.

- Outline links of this literary feature to others.

# Activity 5: Shared Reading Response

**Assessment Criteria:** meaningful and perceptive linking of works
**Description:**

- In small groups students take turns speaking about the last thing that you read - generally the current work.

- The listener is required to ask questions as they go along using the following prompt.

- Both the listener and the speaker need to make note of any questions asked at the end of the activity

**Prompt to assist with questioning**

**As the listener you are required to ask questions related to any of the following:**

- **The speaker's knowledge of the content**

- **How parts of the work relate to the work as a whole and to other works?**

- **What effects literary features have on the reader's response?**

*As a listener you need to help the speaker stay focused and to support their ideas with specific references from the work. Your questioning can help them to do this. The speaker needs to use accurate, clear and precise language. By seeking clarification of points you can help the speaker to do this.*

**Shared Reading Response: Record Sheet for questions asked and responses**

---

### The speaker's knowledge of the content

---

### How parts of the work relate to the work as a whole and to other works?

---

### What effects literary features have on the reader's response?

---

### Other questions

---

## Activity 6: Connecting Theme and Literary Features in a Text

**Assessment Criteria:** in-depth knowledge of, and very good insight into, aspects of the work / purposeful and effective structure / supporting examples are well integrated
**Description:**

- Identify an idea, or theme, expressed through the text you are analyzing.

- Select up to three literary features that appear in the work that in some way support or are related to that identified idea or theme. Highlight these literary features from the given list. Definitions appear in the Vocabulary Log.

- Explain how the chosen literary features support this idea, or theme in the sections below.

- When completing the sections you should attempt to make links between the literary features in terms of how they support each other in the text.

---

# Text:

---

**Theme/Ideas expressed through a text:**

**Literary features identified:**
Allegory, Alliteration, Allusion, Antagonist, Aside, Association, Assonance, Atmosphere, Audience, Blank Verse, Caesura, Caricature, Characterization, Climax, Connotation, Denotation, Denouement, Dialogue, Diction, Enjambment, Euphemism, Flashback, Foreshadowing, Form, Framed Narrative, Free Verse, Genre, Hyperbole, Imagery, Irony, Metaphor, Meter, Metonymy, Mood, Motif, Myth, Narrator, Occasion, Onomatopoeia, Paradox, Parody, Persona, Personification, Plot, Point of View, Protagonist, Repetition, Rhyme, Satire, Setting, Simile, Soliloquy, Sound, Speaker, Structure, Style, Subplot, Subtext, Symbol, Syntax (sentence structure), Theme, Tone

## Literary Feature 1:

**Describe a literary feature that you can identify in your text.**

**Provide specific examples from the text.**

**Describe the effect this literary feature has on the reader/audience.**

**Outline links of this literary feature to other literary features.**

## Literary Feature 2:

**Describe a literary feature that you can identify in your text.**

**Provide specific examples from the text.**

**Describe the effect this literary feature has on the reader/audience.**

**Outline links of this literary feature to other literary features.**

---
## Literary Feature 3:
---

**Describe a literary feature that you can identify in your text.**

**Provide specific examples from the text.**

**Describe the effect this literary feature has on the reader/audience.**

**Outline links of this literary feature to other literary features.**

## Activity 7: Connecting Theme and Literary Features in a Text (Unseen)

**Assessment Criteria:** perceptive understanding of the thought and feeling expressed in the text as well as some of the subtleties of the text / detailed and persuasive references to the text / supporting examples are well integrated / in-depth knowledge of, and very good insight into, aspects of the work / purposeful and effective structure

**Description:** The instructions below are the same as for Activity 6 – you just need to repeat the process for this extract although you may not know the context within which this extract appears. The procedure is exactly the same.

- Identify an idea, or theme, expressed through the text.

- Select an important aspect of the text which supports this theme. Circle this word.

- Identify two literary features that support this aspect of the text. Circle these words.

- Explain how the chosen aspect of the text supports this theme.

- Explain how the chosen literary features support this aspect of the text.

- When you have completed these sections write it all out in one paragraph trying to make the connections as clear as possible.

**Sample extract 4: Martin Luther King, I have a dream; The quotations of Martin Luther King, Jr. (Extract)**

*'I have a dream' by Martin Luther King*
*Delivered on the steps at the Lincoln Memorial in Washington D.C. on August 28, 1963*

And as we walk, we must make the pledge that we shall march ahead. We cannot turn back. There are those who are asking the devotees of civil rights, "When will you be satisfied?" We can never be satisfied as long as our bodies, heavy with the fatigue of travel, cannot gain lodging in the motels of the highways and the hotels of the cities. We cannot be satisfied as long as the Negro's basic mobility is from a smaller ghetto to a larger one. We can never be satisfied as long as a Negro in Mississippi cannot vote and a Negro in New York believes he has nothing for which to vote. No, no, we are not satisfied, and we will not be satisfied until justice rolls down like waters and righteousness like a mighty stream.

I am not unmindful that some of you have come here out of great trials and tribulations. Some of you have come fresh from narrow cells. Some of you have come from areas where your quest for freedom left you battered by the storms of persecution and staggered by the winds of police brutality. You have been the veterans of creative suffering. Continue to work with the faith that unearned suffering is redemptive.

Go back to Mississippi, go back to Alabama, go back to Georgia, go back to Louisiana, go back to the slums and ghettos of our northern cities, knowing that somehow this situation can and will be changed. Let us not wallow in the valley of despair.

I say to you today, my friends, that in spite of the difficulties and frustrations of the moment, I still have a dream. It is a dream deeply rooted in the American dream.

I have a dream that one day this nation will rise up and live out the true meaning of its creed: "We hold these truths to be self-evident: that all men are created equal."

I have a dream that one day on the red hills of Georgia the sons of former slaves and the sons of former slave owners will be able to sit down together at a table of brotherhood.

I have a dream that one day even the state of Mississippi, a desert state, sweltering with the heat of injustice and oppression, will be transformed into an oasis of freedom and justice.

I have a dream that my four children will one day live in a nation where they will not be judged by the color of their skin but by the content of their character.

I have a dream today.

I have a dream that one day the state of Alabama, whose governor's lips are presently dripping with the words of interposition and nullification, will be transformed into a situation where little black boys and black girls will be able to join hands with little white boys and white girls and walk together as sisters and brothers.

I have a dream today.

I have a dream that one day every valley shall be exalted, every hill and mountain shall be made low, the rough places will be made plain, and the crooked places will be made straight, and the glory of the Lord shall be revealed, and all flesh shall see it together.

This is our hope.

This is the faith with which I return to the South. With this faith we will be able to hew out of the mountain of despair a stone of hope. With this faith we will be able to transform the jangling discords of our nation into a beautiful symphony of brotherhood. With this faith we will be able to work together, to pray together, to struggle together, to go to jail together, to stand up for freedom together, knowing that we will be free one day.

(King, 1968)

---

# Text:

---

**Theme/Ideas expressed through this extract:**


**Literary features identified:**

Allegory, Alliteration, Allusion, Antagonist, Aside, Association, Assonance, Atmosphere, Audience, Blank Verse, Caesura, Caricature, Characterization, Climax, Connotation, Denotation, Denouement, Dialogue, Diction, Enjambment, Euphemism, Flashback, Foreshadowing, Form, Framed Narrative, Free Verse, Genre, Hyperbole, Imagery, Irony, Metaphor, Meter, Metonymy, Mood, Motif, Myth, Narrator, Occasion, Onomatopoeia, Paradox, Parody, Persona, Personification, Plot, Point of View, Protagonist, Repetition, Rhyme, Satire, Setting, Simile, Soliloquy, Sound, Speaker, Structure, Style, Subplot, Subtext, Symbol, Syntax (sentence structure), Theme, Tone

---

## Literary Feature 1:

---

**Describe a literary feature in the extract.**

**Provide specific examples from the extract.**

**Describe the effect this literary feature has on the reader/audience.**

**Outline links of this literary feature to other literary features in the extract.**

## Literary Feature 2:

**Describe a literary feature in the extract.**

**Provide specific examples from the extract.**

**Describe the effect this literary feature has on the reader/audience.**

**Outline links of this literary feature to other literary features in the extract.**

## Literary Feature 3:

**Describe a literary feature in the extract.**

**Provide specific examples from the extract.**

**Describe the effect this literary feature has on the reader/audience.**

**Outline links of this literary feature to other literary features in the extract.**

## Activity 8: Analyzing Exam Questions

**Assessment Criteria:** Logical coherence; concise use of language; response to demands of question
**Description:**

- Choose an examination question from the following list. Identify works to which the question will be addressed.

- Identify and highlight the major concepts in the question. These are the words that you think are the most important; the essence of the question.

- Take these words and add some qualifying information showing how these words connect to the chosen works.

- Use these groups of words in your introductory paragraph.

- The words should also appear consistently throughout the rest of your response.

*Remember that exam questions present you with a wide range of possible aspects that you could use as ideas to pursue in other types of assignments such as oral commentaries. Over time this activity will provide you with a bank of ideas to use when analyzing literature.*

## Drama

A dramatist often creates a gap between what the audience knows and what the characters know. With reference to **at least two** plays, discuss how and to what effect dramatists have used this technique.

## Poetry

"A poet would like all parts of a poem—words, lines, stanzas, thoughts, metaphors, rhythms—to work in perfect harmony." To what degree could the poems you studied be considered unified wholes? You must refer to poems from **at least two** poets.

## Prose: The Novel and Short Story

"Defiance becomes our duty in the face of injustice." Referring to **at least two** works you have studied, explore the ways in which the writers have attempted to persuade us to accept or challenge this view.

## Prose: Other than the Novel or Short Story

What are the questions that underlie **at least two** of the works that you have read and how have the authors sought to answer those questions?

## General Questions on Literature

It is said that writers are the conscience of the world. In what ways have **at least two** of the works you have studied encouraged you to appreciate or question this assertion?

"Although doubt is not a pleasant condition, certainty is an absurd one." In the light of this statement, explore the impressions of doubt and/or certainty conveyed in **at least two** works you have studied.

(IB, Paper 2, May 2008 TZ1)

**Highlight the question that you have selected from the list above. In the space below write the words that you have chosen from that question; the essence of the question.**

**Write down your thoughts regarding how these words relate to the work/s that you will be addressing.**

**Based on these thoughts add some qualifying information to the words to show how they connect to the chosen works.**

**Write an introductory paragraph with these words appearing multiple times. Remember that you chose them because they were the essence of the question.**

## Text Five:

*A **Question:** Are you able to answer the questions asked in this activity? If you are having trouble keeping up with the reading you need to see someone who can help you manage your time such as your teacher, a parent or a friend who is managing their workload. On your first reading of the text you will miss a lot of detail. Make sure you allow time for at least one subsequent reading.*

---

## Activity 1: Considering Context

---

**Assessment Criteria:** meaningful and perceptive linking of works / thorough knowledge and understanding of the content of the extract or works

**Description:** Before you start the course you already have a bank of knowledge that will help you to understand the texts. There may also be some misunderstandings that need clearing up.

- Write down notes regarding what you know about the text, author, time period, language or geographic region.

- In pairs share your own information and include new pieces of information from your partner in your workbook.

- During the course when you begin to look at a text as a class bring all your ideas together on the board to both share ideas and dispel misunderstandings.

---

## Text 5

---

**Title:**


**Author:**


**Dates:**


**Country and language of original publication:**


**What do you know about this text, author, time period, language, geographic region or political situation that may be relevant?**

## Activity 2: Quote Bank

**Assessment Criteria:** detailed and persuasive references to the works
**Description:**

- Choose a direct reference from a character in your text. In the case of poetry choose a specific line.
- Comment on the relevance of the reference – what it tells us about the character / poem.
- Finally, comment on the links between these references in terms of their significance for the text as a whole.

---

# Text:

---

**Character One:**

Quote / Reference 1:

Significance:

Quote / Reference 2:

Significance:

Quote / Reference 3:

Significance:

**Comment on the links between these quotes:**

---

# Text:

---

**Character Two:**

Quote / Reference 1:

Significance:

Quote / Reference 2:

Significance:

Quote / Reference 3:

Significance:

**Comment on the links between these quotes:**

## Activity 3: Quote Builder

**Assessment Criteria:** ideas are convincing and show independence of thought
**Description:** Break into small groups or pairs. In turn each group or pair presents a short quote from the text to the opposing team.
The opposing team must supply three pieces of information after hearing the quote:

- Which character the quote is from
- The context in which it appeared in the text
- The significance of the quote for the overall text

The first two have definite answers although the last will be dependent on individual interpretations. All answers that can be justified are acceptable – the language used in the justification of the response is an important aspect of this activity.

## Quote Builder: Round 1 Notes

**Our Quote** (Write it here so you can read it out to the opposition)

**Character:**

**Context:**

**Significance:**

**Opposition Quote** (Just a few notes as you listen to it read out by the opposition)

**Character:**

**Context:**

**Significance:**

## Quote Builder: Round 2 Notes

**Our Quote** (Write it here so you can read it out to the opposition)


**Character:**


**Context:**


**Significance:**


**Opposition Quote** (Just a few notes as you listen to it read out by the opposition)


**Character:**


**Context:**


**Significance:**

## Activity 4: Literary Feature Analysis

**Assessment Criteria:** critical analysis of the effects of the literary features of the works consistently well illustrated by persuasive examples
**Description:**

- Copy a passage from your text into one of the spaces below.

- Identify a literary feature and comment on this feature in the 'Literary features' table.

---

### Copy or paste a short passage from your text here

---

---

## **Literary Feature 1:**

---

- Describe a literary feature that you can see in the passage above.

- Provide specific examples from the text.

- Describe the effect this literary feature has on the reader/audience.

- Outline links of this literary feature to others.

---

## **Literary Feature 2:**

---

- Describe a literary feature that you can see in the passage above.

- Provide specific examples from the text.

- Describe the effect this literary feature has on the reader/audience.

- Outline links of this literary feature to others.

## Literary Feature 3:

- Describe a literary feature that you can see in the passage above.

- Provide specific examples from the text.

- Describe the effect this literary feature has on the reader/audience.

- Outline links of this literary feature to others.

## Literary Feature 4:

- Describe a literary feature that you can see in the passage above.

- Provide specific examples from the text.

- Describe the effect this literary feature has on the reader/audience.

- Outline links of this literary feature to others.

## Activity 5: Shared Reading Response

**Assessment Criteria:** meaningful and perceptive linking of works
**Description:**

- In small groups students take turns speaking about the last thing that you read - generally the current work.
- The listener is required to ask questions as they go along using the following prompt.
- Both the listener and the speaker need to make note of any questions asked at the end of the activity

**Prompt to assist with questioning**

**As the listener you are required to ask questions related to any of the following:**

- **The speaker's knowledge of the content**

- **How parts of the work relate to the work as a whole and to other works?**

- **What effects literary features have on the reader's response?**

*As a listener you need to help the speaker stay focused and to support their ideas with specific references from the work. Your questioning can help them to do this. The speaker needs to use accurate, clear and precise language. By seeking clarification of points you can help the speaker to do this.*

**Shared Reading Response: Record Sheet for questions asked and responses**

## The speaker's knowledge of the content

## How parts of the work relate to the work as a whole and to other works?

## What effects literary features have on the reader's response?

## Other questions

## Activity 6: Connecting Theme and Literary Features in a Text

**Assessment Criteria:** in-depth knowledge of, and very good insight into, aspects of the work / purposeful and effective structure / supporting examples are well integrated
**Description:**

- Identify an idea, or theme, expressed through the text you are analyzing.

- Select up to three literary features that appear in the work that in some way support or are related to that identified idea or theme. Highlight these literary features from the given list. Definitions appear in the Vocabulary Log.

- Explain how the chosen literary features support this idea, or theme in the sections below.

- When completing the sections you should attempt to make links between the literary features in terms of how they support each other in the text.

---

## Text:

---

**Theme/Ideas expressed through a text:**

**Literary features identified:**
Allegory, Alliteration, Allusion, Antagonist, Aside, Association, Assonance, Atmosphere, Audience, Blank Verse, Caesura, Caricature, Characterization, Climax, Connotation, Denotation, Denouement, Dialogue, Diction, Enjambment, Euphemism, Flashback, Foreshadowing, Form, Framed Narrative, Free Verse, Genre, Hyperbole, Imagery, Irony, Metaphor, Meter, Metonymy, Mood, Motif, Myth, Narrator, Occasion, Onomatopoeia, Paradox, Parody, Persona, Personification, Plot, Point of View, Protagonist, Repetition, Rhyme, Satire, Setting, Simile, Soliloquy, Sound, Speaker, Structure, Style, Subplot, Subtext, Symbol, Syntax (sentence structure), Theme, Tone

## Literary Feature 1:

**Describe a literary feature that you can identify in your text.**

**Provide specific examples from the text.**

**Describe the effect this literary feature has on the reader/audience.**

**Outline links of this literary feature to other literary features.**

## Literary Feature 2:

**Describe a literary feature that you can identify in your text.**

**Provide specific examples from the text.**

**Describe the effect this literary feature has on the reader/audience.**

**Outline links of this literary feature to other literary features.**

## Literary Feature 3:

**Describe a literary feature that you can identify in your text.**

**Provide specific examples from the text.**

**Describe the effect this literary feature has on the reader/audience.**

**Outline links of this literary feature to other literary features.**

## Activity 7: Connecting Theme and Literary Features in a Text (Unseen)

**Assessment Criteria:** perceptive understanding of the thought and feeling expressed in the text as well as some of the subtleties of the text / detailed and persuasive references to the text / supporting examples are well integrated / in-depth knowledge of, and very good insight into, aspects of the work / purposeful and effective structure

**Description:** The instructions below are the same as for Activity 6 – you just need to repeat the process for this extract although you may not know the context within which this extract appears. The procedure is exactly the same.

- Identify an idea, or theme, expressed through the text.

- Select an important aspect of the text which supports this theme. Circle this word.

- Identify two literary features that support this aspect of the text. Circle these words.

- Explain how the chosen aspect of the text supports this theme.

- Explain how the chosen literary features support this aspect of the text.

- When you have completed these sections write it all out in one paragraph trying to make the connections as clear as possible.

### Sample extract 5: William Shakespeare: *Othello*

SCENE II. A bedchamber in the castle: DESDEMONA in bed asleep; a light burning.

Enter OTHELLO

OTHELLO

It is the cause, it is the cause, my soul,--
Let me not name it to you, you chaste stars!--
It is the cause. Yet I'll not shed her blood;
Nor scar that whiter skin of hers than snow,
And smooth as monumental alabaster.
Yet she must die, else she'll betray more men.
Put out the light, and then put out the light:
If I quench thee, thou flaming minister,
I can again thy former light restore,
Should I repent me: but once put out thy light,
Thou cunning'st pattern of excelling nature,
I know not where is that Promethean heat
That can thy light relume. When I have pluck'd the rose,
I cannot give it vital growth again.
It must needs wither: I'll smell it on the tree.

Kissing her

Ah balmy breath, that dost almost persuade
Justice to break her sword! One more, one more.
Be thus when thou art dead, and I will kill thee,
And love thee after. One more, and this the last:
So sweet was ne'er so fatal. I must weep,
But they are cruel tears: this sorrow's heavenly;
It strikes where it doth love. She wakes.

DESDEMONA
Who's there? Othello?

OTHELLO
Ay. Desdemona.

DESDEMONA
Will you come to bed, my lord?

OTHELLO
Have you pray'd to-night, Desdemona?

DESDEMONA
Ay, my lord.

OTHELLO
If you bethink yourself of any crime
Unreconciled as yet to heaven and grace,
Solicit for it straight.

DESDEMONA
Alas, my lord, what do you mean by that?

OTHELLO
Well, do it, and be brief; I will walk by:
I would not kill thy unprepared spirit;
No; heaven forfend! I would not kill thy soul.

DESDEMONA
Talk you of killing?

OTHELLO
Ay, I do.

DESDEMONA
Then heaven
Have mercy on me!

OTHELLO
Amen, with all my heart!

DESDEMONA
If you say so, I hope you will not kill me.

OTHELLO
Hum!

DESDEMONA
And yet I fear you; for you are fatal then
When your eyes roll so: why I should fear I know not,
Since guiltiness I know not; but yet I feel I fear.

OTHELLO
Think on thy sins.

DESDEMONA
They are loves I bear to you.

OTHELLO
Ay, and for that thou diest.

DESDEMONA
That death's unnatural that kills for loving.
Alas, why gnaw you so your nether lip?
Some bloody passion shakes your very frame:
These are portents; but yet I hope, I hope,
They do not point on me.

OTHELLO
Peace, and be still!

DESDEMONA
I will so. What's the matter?

OTHELLO
That handkerchief which I so loved and gave thee
Thou gavest to Cassio.

DESDEMONA
No, by my life and soul!
Send for the man, and ask him.

OTHELLO
Sweet soul, take heed,
Take heed of perjury; thou art on thy deathbed.

DESDEMONA
Ay, but not yet to die.

OTHELLO
Yes, presently:
Therefore confess thee freely of thy sin;
For to deny each article with oath
Cannot remove nor choke the strong conception
That I do groan withal. Thou art to die.

DESDEMONA
Then Lord have mercy on me!

OTHELLO
I say, amen.

DESDEMONA
And have you mercy too! I never did
Offend you in my life; never loved Cassio
But with such general warranty of heaven
As I might love: I never gave him token.

(Shakespeare, *Othello*, 2004; originally published approximately 1621)

---

## Text:

---

### Theme/Ideas expressed through this extract:

### Literary features identified:

Allegory, Alliteration, Allusion, Antagonist, Aside, Association, Assonance, Atmosphere, Audience, Blank Verse, Caesura, Caricature, Characterization, Climax, Connotation, Denotation, Denouement, Dialogue, Diction, Enjambment, Euphemism, Flashback, Foreshadowing, Form, Framed Narrative, Free Verse, Genre, Hyperbole, Imagery, Irony, Metaphor, Meter, Metonymy, Mood, Motif, Myth, Narrator, Occasion, Onomatopoeia, Paradox, Parody, Persona, Personification, Plot, Point of View, Protagonist, Repetition, Rhyme, Satire, Setting, Simile, Soliloquy, Sound, Speaker, Structure, Style, Subplot, Subtext, Symbol, Syntax (sentence structure), Theme, Tone

## Literary Feature 1:

**Describe a literary feature in the extract.**

**Provide specific examples from the extract.**

**Describe the effect this literary feature has on the reader/audience.**

**Outline links of this literary feature to other literary features in the extract.**

## Literary Feature 2:

**Describe a literary feature in the extract.**

**Provide specific examples from the extract.**

**Describe the effect this literary feature has on the reader/audience.**

**Outline links of this literary feature to other literary features in the extract.**

## Literary Feature 3:

**Describe a literary feature in the extract.**

**Provide specific examples from the extract.**

**Describe the effect this literary feature has on the reader/audience.**

**Outline links of this literary feature to other literary features in the extract.**

## Activity 8: Analyzing Exam Questions

**Assessment Criteria:** Logical coherence; concise use of language; response to demands of question

**Description:**

- Choose an examination question from the following list. Identify works to which the question will be addressed.

- Identify and highlight the major concepts in the question. These are the words that you think are the most important; the essence of the question.

- Take these words and add some qualifying information showing how these words connect to the chosen works.

- Use these groups of words in your introductory paragraph.

- The words should also appear consistently throughout the rest of your response.

*Remember that exam questions present you with a wide range of possible aspects that you could use as ideas to pursue in other types of assignments such as oral commentaries. Over time this activity will provide you with a bank of ideas to use when analyzing literature.*

## Drama

Most plays have stage directions; some have none or almost none. What do you see as the relevance of stage directions in **at least two** plays you have studied?

## Poetry

"The chief virtue of poetry is not that it appeals to the intellect, but that it opens the imagination and touches the heart." How and to what degree does this view of poetry apply to the works of **at least two** poets you have studied?

## Prose: The Novel and Short Story

Adventure and vivid action are often used to sustain a reader's interest. Explore the ways in which **at least two** writers you have studied have used such means or substituted others to keep the reader reading.

## Prose: Other than the Novel and Short Story

"Communicating truthfully is often the intent of non-fiction." To what extent have **at least two** of the works you have studied convinced you of the validity of the thoughts and feelings expressed by the writer?

## General Questions on Literature

Conversations and interchanges can take place in literature both internally (inside a speaker's head) and externally (with other beings). Discuss ways in which **at least two** writers in your study have used conversations and interchanges to enrich their texts.

In what ways do obsessions or fixations affect writers, speakers, or characters of **at least two** of the works you have studied?

(IB, May 2008, Paper 2, TZ0, Nov 2008, SL)

**Highlight the question that you have selected from the list above. In the space below write the words that you have chosen from that question; the essence of the question.**

**Write down your thoughts regarding how these words relate to the work/s that you will be addressing.**

**Based on these thoughts add some qualifying information to the words to show how they connect to the chosen works.**

**Write an introductory paragraph with these words appearing multiple times. Remember that you chose them because they were the essence of the question.**

# Text Six:

## Activity 1: Considering Context

**Assessment Criteria:** meaningful and perceptive linking of works / thorough knowledge and understanding of the content of the extract or works

**Description:** Before you start the course you already have a bank of knowledge that will help you to understand the texts. There may also be some misunderstandings that need clearing up.

- Write down notes regarding what you know about the text, author, time period, language or geographic region.

- In pairs share your own information and include new pieces of information from your partner in your workbook.

- During the course when you begin to look at a text as a class bring all your ideas together on the board to both share ideas and dispel misunderstandings.

---

## Text 6

---

**Title:**


**Author:**


**Dates:**


**Country and language of original publication:**


**What do you know about this text, author, time period, language, geographic region or political situation that may be relevant?**

## Activity 2: Quote Bank

**Assessment Criteria:** detailed and persuasive references to the works
**Description:**

- Choose a direct reference from a character in your text. In the case of poetry choose a specific line.

- Comment on the relevance of the reference – what it tells us about the character / poem.

- Finally, comment on the links between these references in terms of their significance for the text as a whole.

---

## Text:

---

**Character One:**

Quote / Reference 1:

Significance:

Quote / Reference 2:

Significance:

Quote / Reference 3:

Significance:

**Comment on the links between these quotes:**

---

## Text:

---

**Character Two:**

Quote / Reference 1:

Significance:

Quote / Reference 2:

Significance:

Quote / Reference 3:

Significance:

**Comment on the links between these quotes:**

# Activity 3: Quote Builder

**Assessment Criteria:** ideas are convincing and show independence of thought
**Description:** Break into small groups or pairs. In turn each group or pair presents a short quote from the text to the opposing team.
The opposing team must supply three pieces of information after hearing the quote:

- Which character the quote is from
- The context in which it appeared in the text
- The significance of the quote for the overall text

The first two have definite answers although the last will be dependent on individual interpretations. All answers that can be justified are acceptable – the language used in the justification of the response is an important aspect of this activity.

## Quote Builder: Round 1 Notes

**Our Quote** (Write it here so you can read it out to the opposition)

**Character:**

**Context:**

**Significance:**

**Opposition Quote** (Just a few notes as you listen to it read out by the opposition)

**Character:**

**Context:**

**Significance:**

# Quote Builder: Round 2 Notes

**Our Quote** (Write it here so you can read it out to the opposition)

**Character:**

**Context:**

**Significance:**

**Opposition Quote** (Just a few notes as you listen to it read out by the opposition)

**Character:**

**Context:**

**Significance:**

## Activity 4: Literary Feature Analysis

**Assessment Criteria:** critical analysis of the effects of the literary features of the works consistently well illustrated by persuasive examples

**Description:**

- Copy a passage from your text into one of the spaces below.

- Identify a literary feature and comment on this feature in the 'Literary features' table.

---

### Copy or paste a short passage from your text here

---

## Literary Feature 1:

- Describe a literary feature that you can see in the passage above.


- Provide specific examples from the text.


- Describe the effect this literary feature has on the reader/audience.


- Outline links of this literary feature to others.


## Literary Feature 2:

- Describe a literary feature that you can see in the passage above.


- Provide specific examples from the text.


- Describe the effect this literary feature has on the reader/audience.


- Outline links of this literary feature to others.

## **Literary Feature 3:**

- Describe a literary feature that you can see in the passage above.

- Provide specific examples from the text.

- Describe the effect this literary feature has on the reader/audience.

- Outline links of this literary feature to others.

## **Literary Feature 4:**

- Describe a literary feature that you can see in the passage above.

- Provide specific examples from the text.

- Describe the effect this literary feature has on the reader/audience.

- Outline links of this literary feature to others.

# Activity 5: Shared Reading Response

**Assessment Criteria:** meaningful and perceptive linking of works
**Description:**

- In small groups students take turns speaking about the last thing that you read - generally the current work.

- The listener is required to ask questions as they go along using the following prompt.

- Both the listener and the speaker need to make note of any questions asked at the end of the activity

**Prompt to assist with questioning**

**As the listener you are required to ask questions related to any of the following:**

- **The speaker's knowledge of the content**

- **How parts of the work relate to the work as a whole and to other works?**

- **What effects literary features have on the reader's response?**

*As a listener you need to help the speaker stay focused and to support their ideas with specific references from the work. Your questioning can help them to do this. The speaker needs to use accurate, clear and precise language. By seeking clarification of points you can help the speaker to do this.*

**Shared Reading Response: Record Sheet for questions asked and responses**

## The speaker's knowledge of the content

## How parts of the work relate to the work as a whole and to other works?

## What effects literary features have on the reader's response?

## Other questions

## Activity 6: Connecting Theme and Literary Features in a Text

**Assessment Criteria:** in-depth knowledge of, and very good insight into, aspects of the work / purposeful and effective structure / supporting examples are well integrated

**Description:**

- Identify an idea, or theme, expressed through the text you are analyzing.

- Select up to three literary features that appear in the work that in some way support or are related to that identified idea or theme. Highlight these literary features from the given list. Definitions appear in the Vocabulary Log.

- Explain how the chosen literary features support this idea, or theme in the sections below.

- When completing the sections you should attempt to make links between the literary features in terms of how they support each other in the text.

---

# Text:

---

**Theme/Ideas expressed through a text:**

**Literary features identified:**

Allegory, Alliteration, Allusion, Antagonist, Aside, Association, Assonance, Atmosphere, Audience, Blank Verse, Caesura, Caricature, Characterization, Climax, Connotation, Denotation, Denouement, Dialogue, Diction, Enjambment, Euphemism, Flashback, Foreshadowing, Form, Framed Narrative, Free Verse, Genre, Hyperbole, Imagery, Irony, Metaphor, Meter, Metonymy, Mood, Motif, Myth, Narrator, Occasion, Onomatopoeia, Paradox, Parody, Persona, Personification, Plot, Point of View, Protagonist, Repetition, Rhyme, Satire, Setting, Simile, Soliloquy, Sound, Speaker, Structure, Style, Subplot, Subtext, Symbol, Syntax (sentence structure), Theme, Tone

---

## Literary Feature 1:

---

**Describe a literary feature that you can identify in your text.**

**Provide specific examples from the text.**

**Describe the effect this literary feature has on the reader/audience.**

**Outline links of this literary feature to other literary features.**

## Literary Feature 2:

**Describe a literary feature that you can identify in your text.**

**Provide specific examples from the text.**

**Describe the effect this literary feature has on the reader/audience.**

**Outline links of this literary feature to other literary features.**

---
## Literary Feature 3:
---

**Describe a literary feature that you can identify in your text.**

**Provide specific examples from the text.**

**Describe the effect this literary feature has on the reader/audience.**

**Outline links of this literary feature to other literary features.**

## Activity 7: Connecting Theme and Literary Features in a Text (Unseen)

**Assessment Criteria:** perceptive understanding of the thought and feeling expressed in the text as well as some of the subtleties of the text / detailed and persuasive references to the text / supporting examples are well integrated / in-depth knowledge of, and very good insight into, aspects of the work / purposeful and effective structure

**Description:** The instructions below are the same as for Activity 6 – you just need to repeat the process for this extract although you may not know the context within which this extract appears. The procedure is exactly the same.

- Identify an idea, or theme, expressed through the text.
- Select an important aspect of the text which supports this theme. Circle this word.
- Identify two literary features that support this aspect of the text. Circle these words.
- Explain how the chosen aspect of the text supports this theme.
- Explain how the chosen literary features support this aspect of the text.
- When you have completed these sections write it all out in one paragraph trying to make the connections as clear as possible.

### Sample extract 6: Anita Desai: 'Games at Twilight' in *Games at Twilight*

But Ravi would not let them. He tore himself out of his mother's grasp and pounded across the lawn into their midst, charging at them with his head lowered so that they scattered in surprise. 'I won, I won, I won,' he bawled, shaking his head so that the big tears flew. 'Raghu didn't find me. I won, I won-'

It took them a minute to grasp what he was saying, even who he was. They had quite forgotten him. Raghu had found all the others long ago. There was a fight about who was to be It next. It had been so fierce that their mother had emerged from her bath and made them change to another game. Then they had played another and another. Broken mulberries from the tree and eaten them. Helped the driver wash the car when their father returned from work. Helped the gardener water the beds till he roared at them and swore he would complain to their parents. The parents had come out, taken up their positions on the cane chairs. They had begun to play again, sing and chant. All this time no one had remembered Ravi. Having disappeared from the scene, he had disappeared from their minds. Clean.

'Don't be a fool,' Raghu said roughly, pushing him aside, and even Mira said, 'Stop howling, Ravi. If you want to play, you can stand at the end of the line,' and she put him there very firmly. The game proceeded. Two pairs of arms reached up and met in an arc. The children trooped under it again and again in a lugubrious circle, ducking their heads and intoning

'The grass is green,
The rose is red;
Remember me
When I am dead, dead, dead, dead......'

And the arc of thin arms trembled in the twilight, and the heads were bowed so sadly, and their feet tramped to that melancholy refrain so mournfully, so helplessly, that Ravi could not bear it. He would not follow them, he would not be included in this funeral game. He had wanted victory and triumph—not a funeral. But he had been forgotten, left out and he would not join them now. The ignominy of being forgotten—how could he face it? He felt his heart go heavy and ache inside him unbearably. He lay down full length on the damp grass, crushing his face into it, no longer crying, silenced by a terrible sense of his insignificance.
(Desai, 1998)

---

## Text:

---

**Theme/Ideas expressed through this extract:**

**Literary features identified:**

Allegory, Alliteration, Allusion, Antagonist, Aside, Association, Assonance, Atmosphere, Audience, Blank Verse, Caesura, Caricature, Characterization, Climax, Connotation, Denotation, Denouement, Dialogue, Diction, Enjambment, Euphemism, Flashback, Foreshadowing, Form, Framed Narrative, Free Verse, Genre, Hyperbole, Imagery, Irony, Metaphor, Meter, Metonymy, Mood, Motif, Myth, Narrator, Occasion, Onomatopoeia, Paradox, Parody, Persona, Personification, Plot, Point of View, Protagonist, Repetition, Rhyme, Satire, Setting, Simile, Soliloquy, Sound, Speaker, Structure, Style, Subplot, Subtext, Symbol, Syntax (sentence structure), Theme, Tone

---

## Literary Feature 1:

---

**Describe a literary feature in the extract.**

**Provide specific examples from the extract.**

**Describe the effect this literary feature has on the reader/audience.**

**Outline links of this literary feature to other literary features in the extract.**

---

## Literary Feature 2:

---

**Describe a literary feature in the extract.**

**Provide specific examples from the extract.**

**Describe the effect this literary feature has on the reader/audience.**

**Outline links of this literary feature to other literary features in the extract.**

---

## Literary Feature 3:

---

**Describe a literary feature in the extract.**

**Provide specific examples from the extract.**

**Describe the effect this literary feature has on the reader/audience.**

**Outline links of this literary feature to other literary features in the extract.**

## Activity 8: Analyzing Exam Questions

**Assessment Criteria:** Logical coherence; concise use of language; response to demands of question
**Description:**

- Choose an examination question from the following list. Identify works to which the question will be addressed.

- Identify and highlight the major concepts in the question. These are the words that you think are the most important; the essence of the question.

- Take these words and add some qualifying information showing how these words connect to the chosen works.

- Use these groups of words in your introductory paragraph.

- The words should also appear consistently throughout the rest of your response.

*Remember that exam questions present you with a wide range of possible aspects that you could use as ideas to pursue in other types of assignments such as oral commentaries. Over time this activity will provide you with a bank of ideas to use when analyzing literature.*

## Drama

Plays frequently explore moral or ethical dimensions of choices people make. Discuss in **at least two** plays the dramatic handling of such issues.

## Poetry

"Metaphors work best when they surprise the reader." In light of this statement, consider the effective use of metaphors to convey meaning in the works of **at least two** poets you have studied.

## Prose: The Novel and Short Story

Listening as well as not listening, and even eavesdropping, are all devices which fiction writers use to drive their plots. How have **at least two** writers you have studied used some of these devices in their works, and to what effect?

## Prose: Other than the Novel and Short Story

To what extent have **at least two** writers in your study used material objects (for example a letter, an inherited piece of jewellery or a house) to provide moments or ongoing lines of interest in their work?

## General Questions on Literature

Curiosity can drive characters, reflections, and plots. How have **at least two** writers that you have studied incorporated curiosity into their works, and to what effect?

Honour is often an issue in literary works, whether threatened, defended or lost. How and to what extent has honour been used in **at least two** works you have studied?

(IB, Paper 2, TZ0, Nov 2008, SL)

**Highlight the question that you have selected from the list above. In the space below write the words that you have chosen from that question; the essence of the question.**

**Write down your thoughts regarding how these words relate to the work/s that you will be addressing.**

**Based on these thoughts add some qualifying information to the words to show how they connect to the chosen works.**

**Write an introductory paragraph with these words appearing multiple times. Remember that you chose them because they were the essence of the question.**

# *Text Seven:*

## Activity 1: Considering Context

**Assessment Criteria:** meaningful and perceptive linking of works / thorough knowledge and understanding of the content of the extract or works

**Description:** Before you start the course you already have a bank of knowledge that will help you to understand the texts. There may also be some misunderstandings that need clearing up.

- Write down notes regarding what you know about the text, author, time period, language or geographic region.

- In pairs share your own information and include new pieces of information from your partner in your workbook.

- During the course when you begin to look at a text as a class bring all your ideas together on the board to both share ideas and dispel misunderstandings.

---

## Text 7

---

**Title:**

**Author:**

**Dates:**

**Country and language of original publication:**

**What do you know about this text, author, time period, language, geographic region or political situation that may be relevant?**

## A Reminder

*Are you finding that you are able to incorporate more literature specific terminology into your conversations in class and your writing? These words are used as they have precise meanings and can convey that precise meaning very quickly and very clearly to the listener or reader. They have been created to help you to communicate your ideas. The Vocabulary Log will help you to develop your literature specific terminology.*

## Activity 2: Quote Bank

**Assessment Criteria:** detailed and persuasive references to the works
**Description:**

- Choose a direct reference from a character in your text. In the case of poetry choose a specific line.

- Comment on the relevance of the reference – what it tells us about the character / poem.

- Finally, comment on the links between these references in terms of their significance for the text as a whole.

## Text:

**Character One:**

Quote / Reference 1:

Significance:

Quote / Reference 2:

Significance:

Quote / Reference 3:

Significance:

**Comment on the links between these quotes:**

---

## Text:

---

**Character Two:**

Quote / Reference 1:

Significance:

Quote / Reference 2:

Significance:

Quote / Reference 3:

Significance:

**Comment on the links between these quotes:**

## Activity 3: Quote Builder

**Assessment Criteria:** ideas are convincing and show independence of thought

**Description:** Break into small groups or pairs. In turn each group or pair presents a short quote from the text to the opposing team.

The opposing team must supply three pieces of information after hearing the quote:

- Which character the quote is from
- The context in which it appeared in the text
- The significance of the quote for the overall text

The first two have definite answers although the last will be dependent on individual interpretations. All answers that can be justified are acceptable – the language used in the justification of the response is an important aspect of this activity.

## Quote Builder: Round 1 Notes

**Our Quote** (Write it here so you can read it out to the opposition)

**Character:**

**Context:**

**Significance:**

**Opposition Quote** (Just a few notes as you listen to it read out by the opposition)

**Character:**

**Context:**

**Significance:**

# Quote Builder: Round 2 Notes

**Our Quote** (Write it here so you can read it out to the opposition)

**Character:**

**Context:**

**Significance:**

**Opposition Quote** (Just a few notes as you listen to it read out by the opposition)

**Character:**

**Context:**

**Significance:**

## Activity 4: Literary Feature Analysis

**Assessment Criteria:** critical analysis of the effects of the literary features of the works consistently well illustrated by persuasive examples

**Description:**

- Copy a passage from your text into one of the spaces below.

- Identify a literary feature and comment on this feature in the 'Literary features' table.

---

### Copy or paste a short passage from your text here

---

## Literary Feature 1:

- Describe a literary feature that you can see in the passage above.


- Provide specific examples from the text.


- Describe the effect this literary feature has on the reader/audience.


- Outline links of this literary feature to others.


## Literary Feature 2:

- Describe a literary feature that you can see in the passage above.


- Provide specific examples from the text.


- Describe the effect this literary feature has on the reader/audience.


- Outline links of this literary feature to others.

---

## Literary Feature 3:

---

- Describe a literary feature that you can see in the passage above.


- Provide specific examples from the text.


- Describe the effect this literary feature has on the reader/audience.


- Outline links of this literary feature to others.

---

## Literary Feature 4:

---

- Describe a literary feature that you can see in the passage above.


- Provide specific examples from the text.


- Describe the effect this literary feature has on the reader/audience.


- Outline links of this literary feature to others.

# Activity 5: Shared Reading Response

**Assessment Criteria:** meaningful and perceptive linking of works
**Description:**

- In small groups students take turns speaking about the last thing that you read - generally the current work.

- The listener is required to ask questions as they go along using the following prompt.

- Both the listener and the speaker need to make note of any questions asked at the end of the activity

**Prompt to assist with questioning**

**As the listener you are required to ask questions related to any of the following:**

- **The speaker's knowledge of the content**

- **How parts of the work relate to the work as a whole and to other works?**

- **What effects literary features have on the reader's response?**

*Damian Rentoule*

*As a listener you need to help the speaker stay focused and to support their ideas with specific references from the work. Your questioning can help them to do this. The speaker needs to use accurate, clear and precise language. By seeking clarification of points you can help the speaker to do this.*

**Shared Reading Response: Record Sheet for questions asked and responses**

## The speaker's knowledge of the content

## How parts of the work relate to the work as a whole and to other works?

## What effects literary features have on the reader's response?

## Other questions

## Activity 6: Connecting Theme and Literary Features in a Text

**Assessment Criteria:** in-depth knowledge of, and very good insight into, aspects of the work / purposeful and effective structure / supporting examples are well integrated

**Description:**

- Identify an idea, or theme, expressed through the text you are analyzing.

- Select up to three literary features that appear in the work that in some way support or are related to that identified idea or theme. Highlight these literary features from the given list. Definitions appear in the Vocabulary Log.

- Explain how the chosen literary features support this idea, or theme in the sections below.

- When completing the sections you should attempt to make links between the literary features in terms of how they support each other in the text.

---

# Text:

---

**Theme/Ideas expressed through a text:**

**Literary features identified:**

Allegory, Alliteration, Allusion, Antagonist, Aside, Association, Assonance, Atmosphere, Audience, Blank Verse, Caesura, Caricature, Characterization, Climax, Connotation, Denotation, Denouement, Dialogue, Diction, Enjambment, Euphemism, Flashback, Foreshadowing, Form, Framed Narrative, Free Verse, Genre, Hyperbole, Imagery, Irony, Metaphor, Meter, Metonymy, Mood, Motif, Myth, Narrator, Occasion, Onomatopoeia, Paradox, Parody, Persona, Personification, Plot, Point of View, Protagonist, Repetition, Rhyme, Satire, Setting, Simile, Soliloquy, Sound, Speaker, Structure, Style, Subplot, Subtext, Symbol, Syntax (sentence structure), Theme, Tone

## Literary Feature 1:

**Describe a literary feature that you can identify in your text.**

**Provide specific examples from the text.**

**Describe the effect this literary feature has on the reader/audience.**

**Outline links of this literary feature to other literary features.**

## Literary Feature 2:

**Describe a literary feature that you can identify in your text.**

**Provide specific examples from the text.**

**Describe the effect this literary feature has on the reader/audience.**

**Outline links of this literary feature to other literary features.**

## Literary Feature 3:

**Describe a literary feature that you can identify in your text.**

**Provide specific examples from the text.**

**Describe the effect this literary feature has on the reader/audience.**

**Outline links of this literary feature to other literary features.**

# Activity 7: Connecting Theme and Literary Features in a Text (Unseen)

**Assessment Criteria:** perceptive understanding of the thought and feeling expressed in the text as well as some of the subtleties of the text / detailed and persuasive references to the text / supporting examples are well integrated / in-depth knowledge of, and very good insight into, aspects of the work / purposeful and effective structure

**Description:** The instructions below are the same as for Activity 6 – you just need to repeat the process for this extract although you may not know the context within which this extract appears. The procedure is exactly the same.

Identify an idea, or theme, expressed through the text.

- Select an important aspect of the text which supports this theme. Circle this word.

- Identify two literary features that support this aspect of the text. Circle these words.

- Explain how the chosen aspect of the text supports this theme.

- Explain how the chosen literary features support this aspect of the text.

- When you have completed these sections write it all out in one paragraph trying to make the connections as clear as possible.

### Sample extract 7: George Orwell, *1984*

'You asked me once,' said O'Brien, 'what was in Room 101. I told you that you knew the answer already. Everyone knows it. The thing that is in Room 101 is the worst thing in the world.'

The door opened again. A guard came in, carrying something made of wire, a box or basket of some kind. He set it down on the further table. Because of the position in which O'Brien was standing, Winston could not see what the thing was.

'The worst thing in the world,' said O'Brien, 'varies from individual to individual. It may be burial alive, or death by fire, or by drowning, or by impalement, or fifty other deaths. There are cases where it is some quite trivial thing, not even fatal.'

He had moved a little to one side, so that Winston had a better view of the thing on the table. It was an oblong wire cage with a handle on top for carrying it by. Fixed to the front of it was something that looked like a fencing mask, with the concave side outwards. Although it was three or four metres away from him, he could see that the cage was divided lengthways into two compartments, and that there was some kind of creature in each. They were rats.

'In your case,' said O'Brien, 'the worst thing in the world happens to be rats.'

A sort of premonitory tremor, a fear of he was not certain what, had passed through Winston as soon as he caught his first glimpse of the cage. But at this moment the meaning of the mask-like attachment in front of it suddenly sank into him. His bowels seemed to turn to water.

'You can't do that!' he cried out in a high cracked voice. 'You couldn't, you couldn't! It's impossible.'

'Do you remember,' said O'Brien, 'the moment of panic that used to occur in your dreams? There was a wall of blackness in front of you, and a roaring sound in your ears. There was something terrible on the other side of the wall. You knew that you knew what it was, but you dared not drag it into the open. It was the rats that were on the other side of the wall.'

'O'Brien!' said Winston, making an effort to control his voice. 'You know this is not necessary. What is it that you want me to do?'

O'Brien made no direct answer. When he spoke it was in the schoolmasterish manner that he sometimes affected. He looked thoughtfully into the distance, as though he were addressing an audience somewhere behind Winston's back.

'By itself,' he said, 'pain is not always enough. There are occasions when a human being will stand out against pain, even to the point of death. But for everyone there is something unendurable -- something that cannot be contemplated. Courage and cowardice are not involved. If you are falling from a height it is not cowardly to clutch at a rope. If you have come up from deep water it is not cowardly to fill your lungs with air. It is merely an instinct which cannot be destroyed. It is the same with the rats. For you, they are unendurable. They are a form of pressure that you cannot withstand, even if you wished to. You will do what is required of you.

'But what is it, what is it? How can I do it if I don't know what it is?'

O'Brien picked up the cage and brought it across to the nearer table. He set it down carefully on the baize cloth. Winston could hear the blood singing in his ears. He had the feeling of sitting in utter loneliness. He was in the middle of a great empty plain, a flat desert drenched with sunlight, across which all sounds came to him out of immense distances. Yet the cage with the rats was not two metres away from him. They were enormous rats. They were at the age when a rat's muzzle grows blunt and fierce and his fur brown instead of grey.

'The rat,' said O'Brien, still addressing his invisible audience, 'although a rodent, is carnivorous. You are aware of that. You will have heard of the things that happen in the poor quarters of this town. In some streets a woman dare not leave her baby alone in the house, even for five minutes. The rats are certain to attack it. Within quite a small time they will strip it to the bones. They also attack sick or dying people. They show astonishing intelligence in knowing when a human being is helpless.'

There was an outburst of squeals from the cage. It seemed to reach Winston from far away. The rats were fighting; they were trying to get at each other through the partition. He heard also a deep groan of despair. That, too, seemed to come from outside himself.

'Brien picked up the cage, and, as he did so, pressed something in it. There was a sharp click. Winston made a frantic effort to tear himself loose from the chair. It was hopeless; every part of him, even his head, was held immovably. O'Brien moved the cage nearer. It was less than a metre from Winston's face.

'I have pressed the first lever,' said O'Brien. 'You understand the construction of this cage. The mask will fit over your head, leaving no exit. When I press this other lever, the door of the cage will slide up. These starving brutes will shoot out of it like bullets. Have you ever seen a rat leap through the air? They will leap on to your face and bore straight into it. Sometimes they attack the eyes first. Sometimes they burrow through the cheeks and devour the tongue.'

The cage was nearer; it was closing in. Winston heard a succession of shrill cries which appeared to be occurring in the air above his head. But he fought furiously against his panic. To think, to think, even with a split second left -- to think was the only hope. Suddenly the foul musty odour of the brutes struck his nostrils. There was a violent convulsion of nausea inside him, and he almost lost consciousness. Everything had gone black. For an instant he was insane, a screaming animal. Yet he came out of the blackness clutching an idea. There was one and only one way to save himself. He must interpose another human being, the body of another human being, between himself and the rats.

The circle of the mask was large enough now to shut out the vision of anything else. The wire door was a couple of hand-spans from his face. The rats knew what was coming now. One of them was leaping up and down, the other, an old scaly grandfather of the sewers, stood up, with his pink hands against the bars, and fiercely sniffed the air. Winston could see the whiskers and the yellow teeth. Again the black panic took hold of him. He was blind, helpless, mindless.

'It was a common punishment in Imperial China,' said O'Brien as didactically as ever.

The mask was closing on his face. The wire brushed his cheek. And then -- no, it was not relief, only hope, a tiny fragment of hope. Too late, perhaps too late. But he had suddenly understood that in the whole world there was just one person to whom he could transfer his punishment -- one body that he could thrust between himself and the rats. And he was shouting frantically, over and over.

'Do it to Julia! Do it to Julia! Not me! Julia! I don't care what you do to her. Tear her face off, strip her to the bones. Not me! Julia! Not me!'

(Orwell, *1984*, 2003; originally published 1949)

## Text:

**Theme/Ideas expressed through this extract:**

**Literary features identified:**
Allegory, Alliteration, Allusion, Antagonist, Aside, Association, Assonance, Atmosphere, Audience, Blank Verse, Caesura, Caricature, Characterization, Climax, Connotation, Denotation, Denouement, Dialogue, Diction, Enjambment, Euphemism, Flashback, Foreshadowing, Form, Framed Narrative, Free Verse, Genre, Hyperbole, Imagery, Irony, Metaphor, Meter, Metonymy, Mood, Motif, Myth, Narrator, Occasion, Onomatopoeia, Paradox, Parody, Persona, Personification, Plot, Point of View, Protagonist, Repetition, Rhyme, Satire, Setting, Simile, Soliloquy, Sound, Speaker, Structure, Style, Subplot, Subtext, Symbol, Syntax (sentence structure), Theme, Tone

## Literary Feature 1:

**Describe a literary feature in the extract.**

**Provide specific examples from the extract.**

**Describe the effect this literary feature has on the reader/audience.**

**Outline links of this literary feature to other literary features in the extract.**

## Literary Feature 2:

**Describe a literary feature in the extract.**

**Provide specific examples from the extract.**

**Describe the effect this literary feature has on the reader/audience.**

**Outline links of this literary feature to other literary features in the extract.**

## Literary Feature 3:

**Describe a literary feature in the extract.**

**Provide specific examples from the extract.**

**Describe the effect this literary feature has on the reader/audience.**

**Outline links of this literary feature to other literary features in the extract.**

# Activity 8: Analyzing Exam Questions

**Assessment Criteria:** Logical coherence; concise use of language; response to demands of question
**Description:**

- Choose an examination question from the following list. Identify works to which the question will be addressed.

- Identify and highlight the major concepts in the question. These are the words that you think are the most important; the essence of the question.

- Take these words and add some qualifying information showing how these words connect to the chosen works.

- Use these groups of words in your introductory paragraph.

- The words should also appear consistently throughout the rest of your response.

*Remember that exam questions present you with a wide range of possible aspects that you could use as ideas to pursue in other types of assignments such as oral commentaries. Over time this activity will provide you with a bank of ideas to use when analyzing literature.*

## Drama

The desire for power drives many of the tensions of drama. Discuss the ways in which dramatists have presented tensions which arise from the desire for power in **at least two** plays.

## Poetry

With close reference to **at least two** poets discuss how the opening lines of a poem could be said to anticipate the closing lines.

## Prose: The Novel and Short Story

One expects a novel or short story to have a scene where the protagonist has a moment of revelation and understanding. In what ways have **at least two** writers you have studied presented such moments? How important have they been for one's overall understanding of the work?

## Prose: Other than the Novel and Short Story

The writer's aim is for the reader to reflect, to inquire and to be inspired. How and to what extent have **at least two** writers succeeded in achieving one or more of these aims?

## General Questions on Literature

Literature consists of victors and victims. Discuss how the idea of victors and victims has been presented in **at least two** works you have studied.

Authors can use sickness realistically or metaphorically. Explore the ways in which **at least two** writers have used sickness, and to what effect.

(IB, May 2008, Paper 2, SL, TZ1)

Highlight the question that you have selected from the list above. In the space below write the words that you have chosen from that question; the essence of the question.

Write down your thoughts regarding how these words relate to the work/s that you will be addressing.

Based on these thoughts add some qualifying information to the words to show how they connect to the chosen works.

Write an introductory paragraph with these words appearing multiple times. Remember that you chose them because they were the essence of the question.

# Text Eight:

## A Suggestion

*Do you ever speak about your texts to your parents or guardians, brothers or sister? You could show them the type of questions that are being asked in class using these notes and continue this exercise at home. They will probably surprise you with the questions they ask. Also ask them about their reading – about the ideas coming through their texts and remember that themes or ideas in texts are not restricted to fiction. Apply your developing understanding outside of the classroom with this activity. You will be surprised at what you find out.*

## Activity 1: Considering Context

**Assessment Criteria:** meaningful and perceptive linking of works / thorough knowledge and understanding of the content of the extract or works

**Description:** Before you start the course you already have a bank of knowledge that will help you to understand the texts. There may also be some misunderstandings that need clearing up.

- Write down notes regarding what you know about the text, author, time period, language or geographic region.

- In pairs share your own information and include new pieces of information from your partner in your workbook.

- During the course when you begin to look at a text as a class bring all your ideas together on the board to both share ideas and dispel misunderstandings.

## Text 8

**Title:**

**Author:**

**Dates:**

**Country and language of original publication:**

**What do you know about this text, author, time period, language, geographic region or political situation that may be relevant?**

## Activity 2: Quote Bank

**Assessment Criteria:** detailed and persuasive references to the works
**Description:**

- Choose a direct reference from a character in your text. In the case of poetry choose a specific line.

- Comment on the relevance of the reference – what it tells us about the character / poem.

- Finally, comment on the links between these references in terms of their significance for the text as a whole.

## Text:

**Character One:**

Quote / Reference 1:

Significance:

Quote / Reference 2:

Significance:

Quote / Reference 3:

Significance:

## Comment on the links between these quotes:

---

## Text:

---

**Character Two:**

Quote / Reference 1:

Significance:

Quote / Reference 2:

Significance:

Quote / Reference 3:

Significance:

## Comment on the links between these quotes:

# Activity 3: Quote Builder

**Assessment Criteria:** ideas are convincing and show independence of thought
**Description:** Break into small groups or pairs. In turn each group or pair presents a short quote from the text to the opposing team.
The opposing team must supply three pieces of information after hearing the quote:

- Which character the quote is from
- The context in which it appeared in the text
- The significance of the quote for the overall text

The first two have definite answers although the last will be dependent on individual interpretations. All answers that can be justified are acceptable – the language used in the justification of the response is an important aspect of this activity.

## Quote Builder: Round 1 Notes

**Our Quote** (Write it here so you can read it out to the opposition)

**Character:**

**Context:**

**Significance:**

**Opposition Quote** (Just a few notes as you listen to it read out by the opposition)

**Character:**

**Context:**

**Significance:**

## Quote Builder: Round 2 Notes

**Our Quote** (Write it here so you can read it out to the opposition)

**Character:**

**Context:**

**Significance:**

**Opposition Quote** (Just a few notes as you listen to it read out by the opposition)

**Character:**

**Context:**

**Significance:**

## Activity 4: Literary Feature Analysis

**Assessment Criteria:** critical analysis of the effects of the literary features of the works consistently well illustrated by persuasive examples

**Description:**

- Copy a passage from your text into one of the spaces below.

- Identify a literary feature and comment on this feature in the 'Literary features' table.

---

### Copy or paste a short passage from your text here

---

## Literary Feature 1:

- Describe a literary feature that you can see in the passage above.


- Provide specific examples from the text.


- Describe the effect this literary feature has on the reader/audience.


- Outline links of this literary feature to others.


## Literary Feature 2:

- Describe a literary feature that you can see in the passage above.


- Provide specific examples from the text.


- Describe the effect this literary feature has on the reader/audience.


- Outline links of this literary feature to others.

---

## **Literary Feature 3:**

---

- Describe a literary feature that you can see in the passage above.

- Provide specific examples from the text.

- Describe the effect this literary feature has on the reader/audience.

- Outline links of this literary feature to others.

---

## **Literary Feature 4:**

---

- Describe a literary feature that you can see in the passage above.

- Provide specific examples from the text.

- Describe the effect this literary feature has on the reader/audience.

- Outline links of this literary feature to others.

# Activity 5: Shared Reading Response

**Assessment Criteria:** meaningful and perceptive linking of works
**Description:**

- In small groups students take turns speaking about the last thing that you read - generally the current work.

- The listener is required to ask questions as they go along using the following prompt.

- Both the listener and the speaker need to make note of any questions asked at the end of the activity

**Prompt to assist with questioning**

## As the listener you are required to ask questions related to any of the following:

### The speaker's knowledge of the content

### How parts of the work relate to the work as a whole and to other works?

### What effects literary features have on the reader's response?

*As a listener you need to help the speaker stay focused and to support their ideas with specific references from the work. Your questioning can help them to do this. The speaker needs to use accurate, clear and precise language. By seeking clarification of points you can help the speaker to do this.*

## Shared Reading Response: Record Sheet for questions asked and responses

### The speaker's knowledge of the content

### How parts of the work relate to the work as a whole and to other works?

### What effects literary features have on the reader's response?

### Other questions

# Activity 6: Connecting Theme and Literary Features in a Text

**Assessment Criteria:** in-depth knowledge of, and very good insight into, aspects of the work / purposeful and effective structure / supporting examples are well integrated
**Description:**

- Identify an idea, or theme, expressed through the text you are analyzing.

- Select up to three literary features that appear in the work that in some way support or are related to that identified idea or theme. Highlight these literary features from the given list. Definitions appear in the Vocabulary Log.

- Explain how the chosen literary features support this idea, or theme in the sections below.

- When completing the sections you should attempt to make links between the literary features in terms of how they support each other in the text.

---

## Text:

---

**Theme/Ideas expressed through a text:**

**Literary features identified:**

Allegory, Alliteration, Allusion, Antagonist, Aside, Association, Assonance, Atmosphere, Audience, Blank Verse, Caesura, Caricature, Characterization, Climax, Connotation, Denotation, Denouement, Dialogue, Diction, Enjambment, Euphemism, Flashback, Foreshadowing, Form, Framed Narrative, Free Verse, Genre, Hyperbole, Imagery, Irony, Metaphor, Meter, Metonymy, Mood, Motif, Myth, Narrator, Occasion, Onomatopoeia, Paradox, Parody, Persona, Personification, Plot, Point of View, Protagonist, Repetition, Rhyme, Satire, Setting, Simile, Soliloquy, Sound, Speaker, Structure, Style, Subplot, Subtext, Symbol, Syntax (sentence structure), Theme, Tone

# Literary Feature 1:

**Describe a literary feature that you can identify in your text.**

**Provide specific examples from the text.**

**Describe the effect this literary feature has on the reader/audience.**

**Outline links of this literary feature to other literary features.**

## Literary Feature 2:

**Describe a literary feature that you can identify in your text.**

**Provide specific examples from the text.**

**Describe the effect this literary feature has on the reader/audience.**

**Outline links of this literary feature to other literary features.**

---

## Literary Feature 3:

---

**Describe a literary feature that you can identify in your text.**

**Provide specific examples from the text.**

**Describe the effect this literary feature has on the reader/audience.**

**Outline links of this literary feature to other literary features.**

# Activity 7: Connecting Theme and Literary Features in a Text (Unseen)

**Assessment Criteria:** perceptive understanding of the thought and feeling expressed in the text as well as some of the subtleties of the text / detailed and persuasive references to the text / supporting examples are well integrated / in-depth knowledge of, and very good insight into, aspects of the work / purposeful and effective structure

**Description:** The instructions below are the same as for Activity 6 – you just need to repeat the process for this extract although you may not know the context within which this extract appears. The procedure is exactly the same.

- Identify an idea, or theme, expressed through the text.

- Select an important aspect of the text which supports this theme. Circle this word.

- Identify two literary features that support this aspect of the text. Circle these words.

- Explain how the chosen aspect of the text supports this theme.

- Explain how the chosen literary features support this aspect of the text.

- When you have completed these sections write it all out in one paragraph trying to make the connections as clear as possible.

### Sample extract 8: Sylvia Plath, 'Two Views Of A Cadaver Room' in *The Colossus and Other Poems*

1)

The day she visited the dissecting room
They had four men laid out, black as burnt turkey,
Already half unstrung. A vinegary fume
Of the death vats clung to them;
The white-smocked boys started working.
The head of his cadaver had caved in,
And she could scarcely make out anything
In that rubble of skull plates and old leather.
A sallow piece of string held it together.

In their jars the snail-nosed babies moon and glow.
He hands her the cut-out heart like a cracked heirloom.

*Damian Rentoule*

(2)

In Brueghel's panorama of smoke and slaughter
Two people only are blind to the carrion army:
He, afloat in the sea of her blue satin
Skirts, sings in the direction
Of her bare shoulder, while she bends,
Finger a leaflet of music, over him,
Both of them deaf to the fiddle in the hands
Of the death's-head shadowing their song.
These Flemish lovers flourish; not for long.

Yet desolation, stalled in paint, spares the little country
Foolish, delicate, in the lower right hand corner.

(Plath, 1998)

## Text:

**Theme/Ideas expressed through this extract:**

**Literary features identified:**

Allegory, Alliteration, Allusion, Antagonist, Aside, Association, Assonance, Atmosphere, Audience, Blank Verse, Caesura, Caricature, Characterization, Climax, Connotation, Denotation, Denouement, Dialogue, Diction, Enjambment, Euphemism, Flashback, Foreshadowing, Form, Framed Narrative, Free Verse, Genre, Hyperbole, Imagery, Irony, Metaphor, Meter, Metonymy, Mood, Motif, Myth, Narrator, Occasion, Onomatopoeia, Paradox, Parody, Persona, Personification, Plot, Point of View, Protagonist, Repetition, Rhyme, Satire, Setting, Simile, Soliloquy, Sound, Speaker, Structure, Style, Subplot, Subtext, Symbol, Syntax (sentence structure), Theme, Tone

## Literary Feature 1:

Describe a literary feature in the extract.

Provide specific examples from the extract.

Describe the effect this literary feature has on the reader/audience.

Outline links of this literary feature to other literary features in the extract.

---

## Literary Feature 2:

---

**Describe a literary feature in the extract.**

**Provide specific examples from the extract.**

**Describe the effect this literary feature has on the reader/audience.**

**Outline links of this literary feature to other literary features in the extract.**

---

## Literary Feature 3:

---

**Describe a literary feature in the extract.**

**Provide specific examples from the extract.**

**Describe the effect this literary feature has on the reader/audience.**

**Outline links of this literary feature to other literary features in the extract.**

## Activity 8: Analyzing Exam Questions

**Assessment Criteria:** Logical coherence; concise use of language; response to demands of question
**Description:**

- Choose an examination question from the following list. Identify works to which the question will be addressed.

- Identify and highlight the major concepts in the question. These are the words that you think are the most important; the essence of the question.

- Take these words and add some qualifying information showing how these words connect to the chosen works.

- Use these groups of words in your introductory paragraph.

- The words should also appear consistently throughout the rest of your response.

*Remember that exam questions present you with a wide range of possible aspects that you could use as ideas to pursue in other types of assignments such as oral commentaries. Over time this activity will provide you with a bank of ideas to use when analyzing literature.*

## Drama

"In drama there are more interesting roles for men than for women." Discuss to what extent you agree with this statement and what it is that makes a role interesting. Refer closely to **at least two** plays you have studied.

## Poetry

"Poets are more effective when describing scenes than when describing people." To what extent do you agree with this statement? In what ways have **at least two** poets described either scenes or people, or both?

## Prose: The Novel and Short Story

How, and to what ends, have authors incorporated family relationships into **at least two** works you have studied?

## Prose: Other than the Novel and Short Story

Discuss the ways in which **at least two** authors have created and used surprise as a technique in their writing.

## General Questions on Literature

To what extent, and in what ways, do writers present humans as being dependent on the society they live in? Discuss with reference to **at least two** works that you have studied.

Authors can use sickness realistically or metaphorically. Explore the ways in which **at least two** writers have used sickness, and to what effect.

(IB, May 2008, Paper 2, SL, TZ1)

**Highlight the question that you have selected from the list above. In the space below write the words that you have chosen from that question; the essence of the question.**

**Write down your thoughts regarding how these words relate to the work/s that you will be addressing.**

**Based on these thoughts add some qualifying information to the words to show how they connect to the chosen works.**

**Write an introductory paragraph with these words appearing multiple times. Remember that you chose them because they were the essence of the question.**

*Text Nine:*

**Assessment Criteria:** meaningful and perceptive linking of works / thorough knowledge and understanding of the content of the extract or works

**Description:** Before you start the course you already have a bank of knowledge that will help you to understand the texts. There may also be some misunderstandings that need clearing up.

- Write down notes regarding what you know about the text, author, time period, language or geographic region.

- In pairs share your own information and include new pieces of information from your partner in your workbook.

- During the course when you begin to look at a text as a class bring all your ideas together on the board to both share ideas and dispel misunderstandings.

## Text 9

**Title:**

**Author:**

**Dates:**

**Country and language of original publication:**

**What do you know about this text, author, time period, language, geographic region or political situation that may be relevant?**

## Activity 2: Quote Bank

**Assessment Criteria:** detailed and persuasive references to the works
**Description:**
- 
  - Choose a direct reference from a character in your text. In the case of poetry choose a specific line.
  - Comment on the relevance of the reference – what it tells us about the character / poem.
  - Finally, comment on the links between these references in terms of their significance for the text as a whole.

---

# Text:

---

**Character One:**

Quote / Reference 1:

Significance:

Quote / Reference 2:

Significance:

Quote / Reference 3:

Significance:

**Comment on the links between these quotes:**

## **Text:**

**Character Two:**

Quote / Reference 1:

Significance:

Quote / Reference 2:

Significance:

Quote / Reference 3:

Significance:

## **Comment on the links between these quotes:**

# Activity 3: Quote Builder

**Assessment Criteria:** ideas are convincing and show independence of thought
**Description:** Break into small groups or pairs. In turn each group or pair presents a short quote from the text to the opposing team.
The opposing team must supply three pieces of information after hearing the quote:

- Which character the quote is from
- The context in which it appeared in the text
- The significance of the quote for the overall text

The first two have definite answers although the last will be dependent on individual interpretations. All answers that can be justified are acceptable – the language used in the justification of the response is an important aspect of this activity.

## Quote Builder: Round 1 Notes

**Our Quote** (Write it here so you can read it out to the opposition)


**Character:**


**Context:**


**Significance:**


**Opposition Quote** (Just a few notes as you listen to it read out by the opposition)


**Character:**


**Context:**


**Significance:**

# Quote Builder: Round 2 Notes

**Our Quote** (Write it here so you can read it out to the opposition)

**Character:**

**Context:**

**Significance:**

**Opposition Quote** (Just a few notes as you listen to it read out by the opposition)

**Character:**

**Context:**

**Significance:**

## Activity 4: Literary Feature Analysis

**Assessment Criteria:** critical analysis of the effects of the literary features of the works consistently well illustrated by persuasive examples
**Description:**

- Copy a passage from your text into one of the spaces below.

- Identify a literary feature and comment on this feature in the 'Literary features' table.

---

### Copy or paste a short passage from your text here

---

---

## Literary Feature 1:

---

- Describe a literary feature that you can see in the passage above.


- Provide specific examples from the text.


- Describe the effect this literary feature has on the reader/audience.


- Outline links of this literary feature to others.


---

## Literary Feature 2:

---

- Describe a literary feature that you can see in the passage above.


- Provide specific examples from the text.


- Describe the effect this literary feature has on the reader/audience.


- Outline links of this literary feature to others.

---

## **Literary Feature 3:**

---

- Describe a literary feature that you can see in the passage above.


- Provide specific examples from the text.


- Describe the effect this literary feature has on the reader/audience.


- Outline links of this literary feature to others.

---

## **Literary Feature 4:**

---

- Describe a literary feature that you can see in the passage above.


- Provide specific examples from the text.


- Describe the effect this literary feature has on the reader/audience.


- Outline links of this literary feature to others.

## Activity 5: Shared Reading Response

**Assessment Criteria:** meaningful and perceptive linking of works
**Description:**

- In small groups students take turns speaking about the last thing that you read - generally the current work.

- The listener is required to ask questions as they go along using the following prompt.

- Both the listener and the speaker need to make note of any questions asked at the end of the activity

**Prompt to assist with questioning**

**As the listener you are required to ask questions related to any of the following:**

- **The speaker's knowledge of the content**

- **How parts of the work relate to the work as a whole and to other works?**

- **What effects literary features have on the reader's response?**

*Damian Rentoule*

*As a listener you need to help the speaker stay focused and to support their ideas with specific references from the work. Your questioning can help them to do this. The speaker needs to use accurate, clear and precise language. By seeking clarification of points you can help the speaker to do this.*

**Shared Reading Response: Record Sheet for questions asked and responses**

## The speaker's knowledge of the content

## How parts of the work relate to the work as a whole and to other works?

## What effects literary features have on the reader's response?

## Other questions

## Activity 6: Connecting Theme and Literary Features in a Text

**Assessment Criteria:** in-depth knowledge of, and very good insight into, aspects of the work / purposeful and effective structure / supporting examples are well integrated
**Description:**

- Identify an idea, or theme, expressed through the text you are analyzing.

- Select up to three literary features that appear in the work that in some way support or are related to that identified idea or theme. Highlight these literary features from the given list. Definitions appear in the Vocabulary Log.

- Explain how the chosen literary features support this idea, or theme in the sections below.

- When completing the sections you should attempt to make links between the literary features in terms of how they support each other in the text.

## Text:

**Theme/Ideas expressed through a text:**

**Literary features identified:**
Allegory, Alliteration, Allusion, Antagonist, Aside, Association, Assonance, Atmosphere, Audience, Blank Verse, Caesura, Caricature, Characterization, Climax, Connotation, Denotation, Denouement, Dialogue, Diction, Enjambment, Euphemism, Flashback, Foreshadowing, Form, Framed Narrative, Free Verse, Genre, Hyperbole, Imagery, Irony, Metaphor, Meter, Metonymy, Mood, Motif, Myth, Narrator, Occasion, Onomatopoeia, Paradox, Parody, Persona, Personification, Plot, Point of View, Protagonist, Repetition, Rhyme, Satire, Setting, Simile, Soliloquy, Sound, Speaker, Structure, Style, Subplot, Subtext, Symbol, Syntax (sentence structure), Theme, Tone

---
## Literary Feature 1:
---

**Describe a literary feature that you can identify in your text.**

**Provide specific examples from the text.**

**Describe the effect this literary feature has on the reader/audience.**

**Outline links of this literary feature to other literary features.**

## Literary Feature 2:

**Describe a literary feature that you can identify in your text.**

**Provide specific examples from the text.**

**Describe the effect this literary feature has on the reader/audience.**

**Outline links of this literary feature to other literary features.**

## Literary Feature 3:

**Describe a literary feature that you can identify in your text.**

**Provide specific examples from the text.**

**Describe the effect this literary feature has on the reader/audience.**

**Outline links of this literary feature to other literary features.**

## Activity 7: Connecting Theme and Literary Features in a Text (Unseen)

**Assessment Criteria:** perceptive understanding of the thought and feeling expressed in the text as well as some of the subtleties of the text / detailed and persuasive references to the text / supporting examples are well integrated / in-depth knowledge of, and very good insight into, aspects of the work / purposeful and effective structure

**Description:** The instructions below are the same as for Activity 6 – you just need to repeat the process for this extract although you may not know the context within which this extract appears. The procedure is exactly the same.

- Identify an idea, or theme, expressed through the text.

- Select an important aspect of the text which supports this theme. Circle this word.

- Identify two literary features that support this aspect of the text. Circle these words.

- Explain how the chosen aspect of the text supports this theme.

- Explain how the chosen literary features support this aspect of the text.

- When you have completed these sections write it all out in one paragraph trying to make the connections as clear as possible.

### Sample extract 9: Leo Tolstoy, *War and Peace*

With each fresh blow less and less chance of life remained for those not yet killed. The regiment stood in columns of battalion, three hundred paces apart, but nevertheless the men were always in one and the same mood. All alike were taciturn and morose. Talk was rarely heard in the ranks, and it ceased altogether every time the thud of a successful shot and the cry of "stretchers!" was heard. Most of the time, by their officers' order, the men sat on the ground. One, having taken off his shako, carefully loosened the gathers of its lining and drew them tight again; another, rubbing some dry clay between his palms, polished his bayonet; another fingered the strap and pulled the buckle of his bandolier, while another smoothed and refolded his leg bands and put his boots on again. Some built little houses of the tufts in the plowed ground, or plaited baskets from the straw in the cornfield. All seemed fully absorbed in these pursuits. When men were killed or wounded, when rows of stretchers went past, when some troops retreated, and when great masses of the enemy came into view through the smoke, no one paid any attention to these things. But when our artillery or cavalry advanced or some of our infantry were seen to move forward, words of approval were heard on all sides. But the liveliest attention was attracted by occurrences quite apart from, and unconnected with, the battle. It was as if the minds of these morally exhausted men found relief in everyday, commonplace occurrences. A battery of artillery was passing in front of the regiment. The horse of an ammunition cart put its leg over a trace. "Hey, look at the trace horse!... Get her leg out! She'll fall.... Ah, they don't see it!" came identical shouts from the ranks all along the regiment. Another time, general attention was attracted by a small brown dog, coming heaven knows whence, which trotted in a preoccupied manner in front of the ranks with tail stiffly erect till suddenly a shell fell close by, when it yelped, tucked its tail between its legs, and darted aside. Yells and shrieks of laughter rose from the whole regiment. But such distractions lasted only a moment, and for eight hours the men had been inactive, without food, in constant fear of death, and their pale and gloomy faces grew ever paler and gloomier.

Prince Andrew, pale and gloomy like everyone in the regiment, paced up and down from the border of one patch to another, at the edge of the meadow beside an oat field, with head bowed and arms behind his back. There was nothing for him to do and no orders to be given. Everything went on of itself. The killed were dragged from the front, the wounded carried away, and the ranks closed up. If any soldiers ran to the rear they returned immediately and hastily. At first Prince Andrew, considering it his duty to rouse the courage of the men and to set them an example, walked about among the ranks, but he soon became convinced that this was unnecessary and that there was nothing he could teach them. All the powers of his soul, as of every soldier there, were unconsciously bent on avoiding the contemplation of the horrors of their situation. He walked along the meadow, dragging his feet, rustling the grass, and gazing at the dust that covered his boots; now he took big strides trying to keep to the footprints left on the meadow by the mowers, then he counted his steps, calculating how often he must walk from one strip to another to walk a mile, then he stripped the flowers from the wormwood that grew along a boundary rut, rubbed them in his palms, and smelled their pungent, sweetly bitter scent. Nothing remained of the previous day's thoughts.

He thought of nothing. He listened with weary ears to the ever-recurring sounds, distinguishing the whistle of flying projectiles from the booming of the reports, glanced at the tiresomely familiar faces of the men of the first battalion, and waited. "Here it comes... this one is coming our way again!" he thought, listening to an approaching whistle in the hidden region of smoke. "One, another! Again! It has hit...." He stopped and looked at the ranks. "No, it has gone over. But this one has hit!" And again he started trying to reach the boundary strip in sixteen paces. A whizz and a thud! Five paces from him, a cannon ball tore up the dry earth and disappeared. A chill ran down his back. Again he glanced at the ranks. Probably many had been hit- a large crowd had gathered near the second battalion.

"Adjutant!" he shouted. "Order them not to crowd together."

The adjutant, having obeyed this instruction, approached Prince Andrew. From the other side a battalion commander rode up.

"Look out!" came a frightened cry from a soldier and, like a bird whirring in rapid flight and alighting on the ground, a shell dropped with little noise within two steps of Prince Andrew and close to the battalion commander's horse. The horse first, regardless of whether it was right or wrong to show fear, snorted, reared almost throwing the major, and galloped aside. The horse's terror infected the men.

"Lie down!" cried the adjutant, throwing himself flat on the ground.

Prince Andrew hesitated. The smoking shell spun like a top between him and the prostrate adjutant, near a wormwood plant between the field and the meadow.

"Can this be death?" thought Prince Andrew, looking with a quite new, envious glance at the grass, the wormwood, and the streamlet of smoke that curled up from the rotating black ball. "I cannot, I do not wish to die. I love life- I love this grass, this earth, this air...." He thought this, and at the same time remembered that people were looking at him.

"It's shameful, sir!" he said to the adjutant. "What..."

He did not finish speaking. At one and the same moment came the sound of an explosion, a whistle of splinters as from a breaking window frame, a suffocating smell of powder, and Prince Andrew started to one side, raising his arm, and fell on his chest. Several officers ran up to him. From the right side of his abdomen, blood was welling out making a large stain on the grass.

(Tolstoy, *War and Peace*, 1982; originally published in Russian in 1869)

---

# Text:

---

**Theme/Ideas expressed through this extract:**


**Literary features identified:**

Allegory, Alliteration, Allusion, Antagonist, Aside, Association, Assonance, Atmosphere, Audience, Blank Verse, Caesura, Caricature, Characterization, Climax, Connotation, Denotation, Denouement, Dialogue, Diction, Enjambment, Euphemism, Flashback, Foreshadowing, Form, Framed Narrative, Free Verse, Genre, Hyperbole, Imagery, Irony, Metaphor, Meter, Metonymy, Mood, Motif, Myth, Narrator, Occasion, Onomatopoeia, Paradox, Parody, Persona, Personification, Plot, Point of View, Protagonist, Repetition, Rhyme, Satire, Setting, Simile, Soliloquy, Sound, Speaker, Structure, Style, Subplot, Subtext, Symbol, Syntax (sentence structure), Theme, Tone

## Literary Feature 1:

**Describe a literary feature in the extract.**

**Provide specific examples from the extract.**

**Describe the effect this literary feature has on the reader/audience.**

**Outline links of this literary feature to other literary features in the extract.**

---

## Literary Feature 2:

---

**Describe a literary feature in the extract.**

**Provide specific examples from the extract.**

**Describe the effect this literary feature has on the reader/audience.**

**Outline links of this literary feature to other literary features in the extract.**

## Literary Feature 3:

**Describe a literary feature in the extract.**

**Provide specific examples from the extract.**

**Describe the effect this literary feature has on the reader/audience.**

**Outline links of this literary feature to other literary features in the extract.**

## Activity 8: Analyzing Exam Questions

**Assessment Criteria:** Logical coherence; concise use of language; response to demands of question

**Description:**

- Choose an examination question from the following list. Identify works to which the question will be addressed.

- Identify and highlight the major concepts in the question. These are the words that you think are the most important; the essence of the question.

- Take these words and add some qualifying information showing how these words connect to the chosen works.

- Use these groups of words in your introductory paragraph.

- The words should also appear consistently throughout the rest of your response.

*Remember that exam questions present you with a wide range of possible aspects that you could use as ideas to pursue in other types of assignments such as oral commentaries. Over time this activity will provide you with a bank of ideas to use when analyzing literature.*

## Drama

"On the stage character must be created solely through action, behaviour and speech. "Compare the skill with which dramatists create our impression of the characters in **two** or **three** plays you have studied.

## Poetry

"Imaginary gardens with real toads in them" is one poet's description of poetry. To what extent and with what effect have the poems you studied combined the commonplace with imaginary experience? You must refer closely to the work of **two** or **three** poets in your study and base your answer on a total of **three** or **four** poems.

## Prose: The Novel and Short Story

"The real purpose of fiction is to give pleasure by satisfying the reader's love of the uncommon in human experience… but the uncommonness must be in the events, not in the characters." Discuss how far this 'recipe' for fiction – combining unusual events with recognizable characters – is relevant to **two** or **three** works you have studied.

## Prose: Other than the Novel and Short Story

To what extent and in what ways can the writers of prose other than the novel or short story be seen as advancing new ideas and/or exploring unfamiliar subjects? Support your views with reference to **two** or **three** works you have studied.

## General Questions on Literature

"Some authors prefer to write about 'the real world', while others prefer to be unhindered by the restrictions of reality." Discussing **two** or **three** works, show how the writer's preference helps convey the ideas of the works.

Compare the ways that the treatment of time has been used to shape meaning in **two** or **three** works you have studied.

(IB, November 2006, Paper 2, HL, TZ0)

**Highlight the question that you have selected from the list above. In the space below write the words that you have chosen from that question; the essence of the question.**

**Write down your thoughts regarding how these words relate to the work/s that you will be addressing.**

**Based on these thoughts add some qualifying information to the words to show how they connect to the chosen works.**

**Write an introductory paragraph with these words appearing multiple times. Remember that you chose them because they were the essence of the question.**

## *Text Ten:*

**Assessment Criteria:** meaningful and perceptive linking of works / thorough knowledge and understanding of the content of the extract or works

**Description:** Before you start the course you already have a bank of knowledge that will help you to understand the texts. There may also be some misunderstandings that need clearing up.

- Write down notes regarding what you know about the text, author, time period, language or geographic region.

- In pairs share your own information and include new pieces of information from your partner in your workbook.

- During the course when you begin to look at a text as a class bring all your ideas together on the board to both share ideas and dispel misunderstandings.

## Text 10

**Title:**

**Author:**

**Dates:**

**Country and language of original publication:**

**What do you know about this text, author, time period, language, geographic region or political situation that may be relevant?**

## Activity 2: Quote Bank

**Assessment Criteria:** detailed and persuasive references to the works
**Description:**

- Choose a direct reference from a character in your text. In the case of poetry choose a specific line.
- Comment on the relevance of the reference – what it tells us about the character / poem.
- Finally, comment on the links between these references in terms of their significance for the text as a whole.

---

# Text:

---

**Character One:**

Quote / Reference 1:

Significance:

Quote / Reference 2:

Significance:

Quote / Reference 3:

Significance:

**Comment on the links between these quotes:**

---

**Text:**

---

**Character Two:**

Quote / Reference 1:

Significance:

Quote / Reference 2:

Significance:

Quote / Reference 3:

Significance:

**Comment on the links between these quotes:**

# Activity 3: Quote Builder

**Assessment Criteria:** ideas are convincing and show independence of thought
**Description:** Break into small groups or pairs. In turn each group or pair presents a short quote from the text to the opposing team.
The opposing team must supply three pieces of information after hearing the quote:

- Which character the quote is from
- The context in which it appeared in the text
- The significance of the quote for the overall text

The first two have definite answers although the last will be dependent on individual interpretations. All answers that can be justified are acceptable – the language used in the justification of the response is an important aspect of this activity.

## Quote Builder: Round 1 Notes

**Our Quote** (Write it here so you can read it out to the opposition)

**Character:**

**Context:**

**Significance:**

**Opposition Quote** (Just a few notes as you listen to it read out by the opposition)

**Character:**

**Context:**

**Significance:**

# Quote Builder: Round 2 Notes

**Our Quote** (Write it here so you can read it out to the opposition)

**Character:**

**Context:**

**Significance:**

**Opposition Quote** (Just a few notes as you listen to it read out by the opposition)

**Character:**

**Context:**

**Significance:**

## Activity 4: Literary Feature Analysis

**Assessment Criteria:** *critical analysis of the effects of the literary features of the works consistently well illustrated by persuasive examples*

**Description:**

- Copy a passage from your text into one of the spaces below.

- Identify a literary feature and comment on this feature in the 'Literary features' table.

## Copy or paste a short passage from your text here

## Literary Feature 1:

- Describe a literary feature that you can see in the passage above.

- Provide specific examples from the text.

- Describe the effect this literary feature has on the reader/audience.

- Outline links of this literary feature to others.

## Literary Feature 2:

- Describe a literary feature that you can see in the passage above.

- Provide specific examples from the text.

- Describe the effect this literary feature has on the reader/audience.

- Outline links of this literary feature to others.

## Literary Feature 3:

- Describe a literary feature that you can see in the passage above.

- Provide specific examples from the text.

- Describe the effect this literary feature has on the reader/audience.

- Outline links of this literary feature to others.

## Literary Feature 4:

- Describe a literary feature that you can see in the passage above.

- Provide specific examples from the text.

- Describe the effect this literary feature has on the reader/audience.

- Outline links of this literary feature to others.

# Activity 5: Shared Reading Response

**Assessment Criteria:** meaningful and perceptive linking of works
**Description:**

- In small groups students take turns speaking about the last thing that you read - generally the current work.

- The listener is required to ask questions as they go along using the following prompt.

- Both the listener and the speaker need to make note of any questions asked at the end of the activity

**Prompt to assist with questioning**

**As the listener you are required to ask questions related to any of the following:**

- **The speaker's knowledge of the content**

- **How parts of the work relate to the work as a whole and to other works?**

- **What effects literary features have on the reader's response?**

*As a listener you need to help the speaker stay focused and to support their ideas with specific references from the work. Your questioning can help them to do this. The speaker needs to use accurate, clear and precise language. By seeking clarification of points you can help the speaker to do this.*

**Shared Reading Response: Record Sheet for questions asked and responses**

## The speaker's knowledge of the content

## How parts of the work relate to the work as a whole and to other works?

## What effects literary features have on the reader's response?

## Other questions

## Activity 6: Connecting Theme and Literary Features in a Text

**Assessment Criteria:** in-depth knowledge of, and very good insight into, aspects of the work / purposeful and effective structure / supporting examples are well integrated

**Description:**

- Identify an idea, or theme, expressed through the text you are analyzing.

- Select up to three literary features that appear in the work that in some way support or are related to that identified idea or theme. Highlight these literary features from the given list. Definitions appear in the Vocabulary Log.

- Explain how the chosen literary features support this idea, or theme in the sections below.

- When completing the sections you should attempt to make links between the literary features in terms of how they support each other in the text.

---

# Text:

---

**Theme/Ideas expressed through a text:**

**Literary features identified:**

Allegory, Alliteration, Allusion, Antagonist, Aside, Association, Assonance, Atmosphere, Audience, Blank Verse, Caesura, Caricature, Characterization, Climax, Connotation, Denotation, Denouement, Dialogue, Diction, Enjambment, Euphemism, Flashback, Foreshadowing, Form, Framed Narrative, Free Verse, Genre, Hyperbole, Imagery, Irony, Metaphor, Meter, Metonymy, Mood, Motif, Myth, Narrator, Occasion, Onomatopoeia, Paradox, Parody, Persona, Personification, Plot, Point of View, Protagonist, Repetition, Rhyme, Satire, Setting, Simile, Soliloquy, Sound, Speaker, Structure, Style, Subplot, Subtext, Symbol, Syntax (sentence structure), Theme, Tone

## Literary Feature 1:

**Describe a literary feature that you can identify in your text.**

**Provide specific examples from the text.**

**Describe the effect this literary feature has on the reader/audience.**

**Outline links of this literary feature to other literary features.**

## Literary Feature 2:

**Describe a literary feature that you can identify in your text.**

**Provide specific examples from the text.**

**Describe the effect this literary feature has on the reader/audience.**

**Outline links of this literary feature to other literary features.**

## Literary Feature 3:

**Describe a literary feature that you can identify in your text.**

**Provide specific examples from the text.**

**Describe the effect this literary feature has on the reader/audience.**

**Outline links of this literary feature to other literary features.**

## Activity 7: Connecting Theme and Literary Features in a Text (Unseen)

**Assessment Criteria:** perceptive understanding of the thought and feeling expressed in the text as well as some of the subtleties of the text / detailed and persuasive references to the text / supporting examples are well integrated / in-depth knowledge of, and very good insight into, aspects of the work / purposeful and effective structure

**Description:** The instructions below are the same as for Activity 6 – you just need to repeat the process for this extract although you may not know the context within which this extract appears. The procedure is exactly the same.

- Identify an idea, or theme, expressed through the text.

- Select an important aspect of the text which supports this theme. Circle this word.

- Identify two literary features that support this aspect of the text. Circle these words.

- Explain how the chosen aspect of the text supports this theme.

- Explain how the chosen literary features support this aspect of the text.

- When you have completed these sections write it all out in one paragraph trying to make the connections as clear as possible.

### Sample extract 10: Jonathan Swift: 'A Modest Proposal' in *A Modest Proposal and Other Satires*

It is a melancholy object to those who walk through this great town or travel in the country, when they see the streets, the roads, and cabin doors, crowded with beggars of the female sex, followed by three, four, or six children, all in rags and importuning every passenger for an alms. These mothers, instead of being able to work for their honest livelihood, are forced to employ all their time in strolling to beg sustenance for their helpless infants: who as they grow up either turn thieves for want of work, or leave their dear native country to fight for the Pretender in Spain, or sell themselves to the Barbadoes.

I think it is agreed by all parties that this prodigious number of children in the arms, or on the backs, or at the heels of their mothers, and frequently of their fathers, is in the present deplorable state of the kingdom a very great additional grievance; and, therefore, whoever could find out a fair, cheap, and easy method of making these children sound, useful members of the commonwealth, would deserve so well of the public as to have his statue set up for a preserver of the nation.

But my intention is very far from being confined to provide only for the children of professed beggars; it is of a much greater extent, and shall take in the whole number of infants at a certain age who are born of parents in effect as little able to support them as those who demand our charity in the streets.

As to my own part, having turned my thoughts for many years upon this important subject, and maturely weighed the several schemes of other projectors, I have always found them grossly mistaken in the computation. It is true, a child just dropped from its dam may be supported by her milk for a solar year, with little other nourishment; at most not above the value of 2s., which the mother may certainly get, or the value in scraps, by her lawful occupation of begging; and it is exactly at one year old that I propose to provide for them in such a manner as instead of being a charge upon their parents or the parish, or wanting food and raiment for the rest of their lives, they shall on the contrary contribute to the feeding, and partly to the clothing, of many thousands.

There is likewise another great advantage in my scheme, that it will prevent those voluntary abortions, and that horrid practice of women murdering their bastard children, alas! too frequent among us! sacrificing the poor innocent babes I doubt more to avoid the expense than the shame, which would move tears and pity in the most savage and inhuman breast.

The number of souls in this kingdom being usually reckoned one million and a half, of these I calculate there may be about two hundred thousand couple whose wives are breeders; from which number I subtract thirty thousand couples who are able to maintain their own children, although I apprehend there cannot be so many, under the present distresses of the kingdom; but this being granted, there will remain an hundred and seventy thousand breeders. I again subtract fifty thousand for those women who miscarry, or whose children die by accident or disease within the year. There only remains one hundred and twenty thousand children of poor parents annually born: the question therefore is, how this number shall be reared and provided for, which, as I have already said, under the present situation of affairs, is utterly impossible by all the methods hitherto proposed. For we can neither employ them in handicraft or agriculture; we neither build houses (I mean in the country) nor cultivate land: they can very seldom pick up a livelihood by stealing, till they arrive at six years old, except where they are of towardly parts, although I confess they learn the rudiments much earlier, during which time, they can however be properly looked upon only as probationers, as I have been informed by a principal gentleman in the county of Cavan, who protested to me that he never knew above one or two instances under the age of six, even in a part of the kingdom so renowned for the quickest proficiency in that art.

I am assured by our merchants, that a boy or a girl before twelve years old is no salable commodity; and even when they come to this age they will not yield above three pounds, or three pounds and half-a-crown at most on the exchange; which cannot turn to account either to the parents or kingdom, the charge of nutriment and rags having been at least four times that value.

I shall now therefore humbly propose my own thoughts, which I hope will not be liable to the least objection.

I have been assured by a very knowing American of my acquaintance in London, that a young healthy child well nursed is at a year old a most delicious, nourishing, and wholesome food, whether stewed, roasted, baked, or boiled; and I make no doubt that it will equally serve in a fricassee or a ragout...

(Swift, *A Modest Proposal and Other Satires* , 1995; originally published in 1729)

## Text:

**Theme/Ideas expressed through this extract:**

**Literary features identified:**

Allegory, Alliteration, Allusion, Antagonist, Aside, Association, Assonance, Atmosphere, Audience, Blank Verse, Caesura, Caricature, Characterization, Climax, Connotation, Denotation, Denouement, Dialogue, Diction, Enjambment, Euphemism, Flashback, Foreshadowing, Form, Framed Narrative, Free Verse, Genre, Hyperbole, Imagery, Irony, Metaphor, Meter, Metonymy, Mood, Motif, Myth, Narrator, Occasion, Onomatopoeia, Paradox, Parody, Persona, Personification, Plot, Point of View, Protagonist, Repetition, Rhyme, Satire, Setting, Simile, Soliloquy, Sound, Speaker, Structure, Style, Subplot, Subtext, Symbol, Syntax (sentence structure), Theme, Tone

## Literary Feature 1:

**Describe a literary feature in the extract.**

**Provide specific examples from the extract.**

**Describe the effect this literary feature has on the reader/audience.**

**Outline links of this literary feature to other literary features in the extract.**

---

## Literary Feature 2:

---

**Describe a literary feature in the extract.**

**Provide specific examples from the extract.**

**Describe the effect this literary feature has on the reader/audience.**

**Outline links of this literary feature to other literary features in the extract.**

## Literary Feature 3:

**Describe a literary feature in the extract.**

**Provide specific examples from the extract.**

**Describe the effect this literary feature has on the reader/audience.**

**Outline links of this literary feature to other literary features in the extract.**

## Activity 8: Analyzing Exam Questions

**Assessment Criteria:** Logical coherence; concise use of language; response to demands of question

**Description:**

- Choose an examination question from the following list. Identify works to which the question will be addressed.

- Identify and highlight the major concepts in the question. These are the words that you think are the most important; the essence of the question.

- Take these words and add some qualifying information showing how these words connect to the chosen works.

- Use these groups of words in your introductory paragraph.

- The words should also appear consistently throughout the rest of your response.

*Remember that exam questions present you with a wide range of possible aspects that you could use as ideas to pursue in other types of assignments such as oral commentaries. Over time this activity will provide you with a bank of ideas to use when analyzing literature.*

## Drama

"All plays pose questions about the world, yet some questions are easier to ignore than others." In the light of this statement, evaluate the questions raised in **two** or **three** plays and show how and to what degree these issues are explored.

## Poetry

A poem – whatever else it may be – is a self-contained construct with a life of its own. "Considering both content and form, how far do you agree with this statement? You must refer closely to the work of **two** or **three** poets in your study and base your answer on a total of **three** or **four** poems.

## Prose: The Novel and Short Story

Evaluate the effectiveness of devices used to represent internal states of mind in **two** or **three** works of fiction you have studied.

## Prose: Other than the Novel and Short Story

The attitude a writer takes to his or her materials has a significant effect on the way readers perceive or appreciate them. Discuss the effect of varying attitudes toward the writer's subjects in **two** or **three** works other than the novel or short story.

## General Questions on Literature

In what ways and to what effect have writers in your study made it possible for you to choose more than one interpretation of their works? Use **two** or **three** works you have studied in your answer.

"Mirror or X-Ray or lamp?" Which of these terms do you think best describes the way writers in your study have represented the world? In each case examine how this effect is achieved, using **two** or **three** works you have studied.

(IB, November 2006, Paper 2, HL, TZ0)

**Highlight the question that you have selected from the list above. In the space below write the words that you have chosen from that question; the essence of the question.**

**Write down your thoughts regarding how these words relate to the work/s that you will be addressing.**

**Based on these thoughts add some qualifying information to the words to show how they connect to the chosen works.**

**Write an introductory paragraph with these words appearing multiple times. Remember that you chose them because they were the essence of the question.**

*Text Eleven:*

**Assessment Criteria:** meaningful and perceptive linking of works / thorough knowledge and understanding of the content of the extract or works

**Description:** Before you start the course you already have a bank of knowledge that will help you to understand the texts. There may also be some misunderstandings that need clearing up.

- Write down notes regarding what you know about the text, author, time period, language or geographic region.

- In pairs share your own information and include new pieces of information from your partner in your workbook.

- During the course when you begin to look at a text as a class bring all your ideas together on the board to both share ideas and dispel misunderstandings.

## Text 11

**Title:**

**Author:**

**Dates:**

**Country and language of original publication:**

**What do you know about this text, author, time period, language, geographic region or political situation that may be relevant?**

## Activity 2: Quote Bank

**Assessment Criteria:** detailed and persuasive references to the works
**Description:**

- Choose a direct reference from a character in your text. In the case of poetry choose a specific line.
- Comment on the relevance of the reference – what it tells us about the character / poem.
- Finally, comment on the links between these references in terms of their significance for the text as a whole.

## Text:

**Character One:**

Quote / Reference 1:

Significance:

Quote / Reference 2:

Significance:

Quote / Reference 3:

Significance:

**Comment on the links between these quotes:**

## Text:

**Character Two:**

Quote / Reference 1:

Significance:

Quote / Reference 2:

Significance:

Quote / Reference 3:

Significance:

**Comment on the links between these quotes:**

## Activity 3: Quote Builder

**Assessment Criteria:** ideas are convincing and show independence of thought
**Description:** Break into small groups or pairs. In turn each group or pair presents a short quote from the text to the opposing team.
The opposing team must supply three pieces of information after hearing the quote:

- Which character the quote is from
- The context in which it appeared in the text
- The significance of the quote for the overall text

The first two have definite answers although the last will be dependent on individual interpretations. All answers that can be justified are acceptable – the language used in the justification of the response is an important aspect of this activity.

## Quote Builder: Round 1 Notes

**Our Quote** (Write it here so you can read it out to the opposition)

**Character:**

**Context:**

**Significance:**

**Opposition Quote** (Just a few notes as you listen to it read out by the opposition)

**Character:**

**Context:**

**Significance:**

# Quote Builder: Round 2 Notes

**Our Quote** (Write it here so you can read it out to the opposition)

**Character:**

**Context:**

**Significance:**

**Opposition Quote** (Just a few notes as you listen to it read out by the opposition)

**Character:**

**Context:**

**Significance:**

## Activity 4: Literary Feature Analysis

**Assessment Criteria:** *critical analysis of the effects of the literary features of the works consistently well illustrated by persuasive examples*

**Description:**

- Copy a passage from your text into one of the spaces below.

- Identify a literary feature and comment on this feature in the 'Literary features' table.

---

### Copy or paste a short passage from your text here

---

## Literary Feature 1:

- Describe a literary feature that you can see in the passage above.

- Provide specific examples from the text.

- Describe the effect this literary feature has on the reader/audience.

- Outline links of this literary feature to others.

## Literary Feature 2:

- Describe a literary feature that you can see in the passage above.

- Provide specific examples from the text.

- Describe the effect this literary feature has on the reader/audience.

- Outline links of this literary feature to others.

---
## **Literary Feature 3:**
---

- Describe a literary feature that you can see in the passage above.


- Provide specific examples from the text.


- Describe the effect this literary feature has on the reader/audience.


- Outline links of this literary feature to others.

---
## **Literary Feature 4:**
---

- Describe a literary feature that you can see in the passage above.


- Provide specific examples from the text.


- Describe the effect this literary feature has on the reader/audience.


- Outline links of this literary feature to others.

## Activity 5: Shared Reading Response

**Assessment Criteria:** meaningful and perceptive linking of works
**Description:**

- In small groups students take turns speaking about the last thing that you read - generally the current work.

- The listener is required to ask questions as they go along using the following prompt.

- Both the listener and the speaker need to make note of any questions asked at the end of the activity

**Prompt to assist with questioning**

---

# As the listener you are required to ask questions related to any of the following:

---

### The speaker's knowledge of the content

---

### How parts of the work relate to the work as a whole and to other works?

---

### What effects literary features have on the reader's response?

---

*As a listener you need to help the speaker stay focused and to support their ideas with specific references from the work. Your questioning can help them to do this. The speaker needs to use accurate, clear and precise language. By seeking clarification of points you can help the speaker to do this.*

**Shared Reading Response: Record Sheet for questions asked and responses**

**The speaker's knowledge of the content**

**How parts of the work relate to the work as a whole and to other works?**

**What effects literary features have on the reader's response?**

**Other questions**

## Activity 6: Connecting Theme and Literary Features in a Text

**Assessment Criteria:** in-depth knowledge of, and very good insight into, aspects of the work / purposeful and effective structure / supporting examples are well integrated
**Description:**

- Identify an idea, or theme, expressed through the text you are analyzing.

- Select up to three literary features that appear in the work that in some way support or are related to that identified idea or theme. Highlight these literary features from the given list. Definitions appear in the Vocabulary Log.

- Explain how the chosen literary features support this idea, or theme in the sections below.

- When completing the sections you should attempt to make links between the literary features in terms of how they support each other in the text.

---

# Text:

---

**Theme/Ideas expressed through a text:**

**Literary features identified:**
Allegory, Alliteration, Allusion, Antagonist, Aside, Association, Assonance, Atmosphere, Audience, Blank Verse, Caesura, Caricature, Characterization, Climax, Connotation, Denotation, Denouement, Dialogue, Diction, Enjambment, Euphemism, Flashback, Foreshadowing, Form, Framed Narrative, Free Verse, Genre, Hyperbole, Imagery, Irony, Metaphor, Meter, Metonymy, Mood, Motif, Myth, Narrator, Occasion, Onomatopoeia, Paradox, Parody, Persona, Personification, Plot, Point of View, Protagonist, Repetition, Rhyme, Satire, Setting, Simile, Soliloquy, Sound, Speaker, Structure, Style, Subplot, Subtext, Symbol, Syntax (sentence structure), Theme, Tone

---

## Literary Feature 1:

---

**Describe a literary feature that you can identify in your text.**

**Provide specific examples from the text.**

**Describe the effect this literary feature has on the reader/audience.**

**Outline links of this literary feature to other literary features.**

## Literary Feature 2:

**Describe a literary feature that you can identify in your text.**

**Provide specific examples from the text.**

**Describe the effect this literary feature has on the reader/audience.**

**Outline links of this literary feature to other literary features.**

---

## Literary Feature 3:

---

**Describe a literary feature that you can identify in your text.**

**Provide specific examples from the text.**

**Describe the effect this literary feature has on the reader/audience.**

**Outline links of this literary feature to other literary features.**

## Activity 7: Connecting Theme and Literary Features in a Text (Unseen)

**Assessment Criteria:** perceptive understanding of the thought and feeling expressed in the text as well as some of the subtleties of the text / detailed and persuasive references to the text / supporting examples are well integrated / in-depth knowledge of, and very good insight into, aspects of the work / purposeful and effective structure

**Description:** The instructions below are the same as for Activity 6 – you just need to repeat the process for this extract although you may not know the context within which this extract appears. The procedure is exactly the same.

- Identify an idea, or theme, expressed through the text.

- Select an important aspect of the text which supports this theme. Circle this word.

- Identify two literary features that support this aspect of the text. Circle these words.

- Explain how the chosen aspect of the text supports this theme.

- Explain how the chosen literary features support this aspect of the text.

- When you have completed these sections write it all out in one paragraph trying to make the connections as clear as possible.

### Sample extract 11: Joseph Conrad: *Heart of Darkness*

"Black shapes crouched, lay, sat between the trees leaning against the trunks, clinging to the earth, half coming out, half effaced within the dim light, in all the attitudes of pain, abandonment, and despair. Another mine on the cliff went off, followed by a slight shudder of the soil under my feet. The work was going on. The work! And this was the place where some of the helpers had withdrawn to die.

"They were dying slowly--it was very clear. They were not enemies, they were not criminals, they were nothing earthly now-- nothing but black shadows of disease and starvation, lying confusedly in the greenish gloom. Brought from all the recesses of the coast in all the legality of time contracts, lost in uncongenial surroundings, fed on unfamiliar food, they sickened, became inefficient, and were then allowed to crawl away and rest. These moribund shapes were free as air--and nearly as thin. I began to distinguish the gleam of the eyes under the trees. Then, glancing down, I saw a face near my hand. The black bones reclined at full length with one shoulder against the tree, and slowly the eyelids rose and the sunken eyes looked up at me, enormous and vacant, a kind of blind, white flicker in the depths of the orbs, which died out slowly. The man seemed young-- almost a boy--but you know with them it's hard to tell. I found nothing else to do but to offer him one of my good Swede's ship's biscuits I had in my pocket. The fingers closed slowly on it and held--there was no other movement and no other glance. He had tied a bit of white worsted round his neck--Why? Where did he get it? Was it a badge--an ornament--a charm-- a propitiatory act? Was there any idea at all connected with it? It looked startling round his black neck, this bit of white thread from beyond the seas.

"Near the same tree two more bundles of acute angles sat with their legs drawn up. One, with his chin propped on his knees, stared at nothing, in an intolerable and appalling manner: his brother phantom rested its forehead, as if overcome with a great weariness; and all about others were scattered in every pose of contorted collapse, as in some picture of a massacre or a pestilence. While I stood horror-struck, one of these creatures rose to his hands and knees, and went off on all-fours towards the river to drink. He lapped out of his hand, then sat up in the sunlight, crossing his shins in front of him, and after a time let his woolly head fall on his breastbone.

"I didn't want any more loitering in the shade, and I made haste towards the station. When near the buildings I met a white man, in such an unexpected elegance of get-up that in the first moment I took him for a sort of vision. I saw a high starched collar, white cuffs, a light alpaca jacket, snowy trousers, a clean necktie, and varnished boots. No hat. Hair parted, brushed, oiled, under a green-lined parasol held in a big white hand. He was amazing, and had a penholder behind his ear.

"I shook hands with this miracle ....."

(Conrad, 2002; originally published in 1899)

## Text:

**Theme/Ideas expressed through this extract:**

**Literary features identified:**

Allegory, Alliteration, Allusion, Antagonist, Aside, Association, Assonance, Atmosphere, Audience, Blank Verse, Caesura, Caricature, Characterization, Climax, Connotation, Denotation, Denouement, Dialogue, Diction, Enjambment, Euphemism, Flashback, Foreshadowing, Form, Framed Narrative, Free Verse, Genre, Hyperbole, Imagery, Irony, Metaphor, Meter, Metonymy, Mood, Motif, Myth, Narrator, Occasion, Onomatopoeia, Paradox, Parody, Persona, Personification, Plot, Point of View, Protagonist, Repetition, Rhyme, Satire, Setting, Simile, Soliloquy, Sound, Speaker, Structure, Style, Subplot, Subtext, Symbol, Syntax (sentence structure), Theme, Tone

---

## Literary Feature 1:

---

**Describe a literary feature in the extract.**

**Provide specific examples from the extract.**

**Describe the effect this literary feature has on the reader/audience.**

**Outline links of this literary feature to other literary features in the extract.**

## Literary Feature 2:

**Describe a literary feature in the extract.**

**Provide specific examples from the extract.**

**Describe the effect this literary feature has on the reader/audience.**

**Outline links of this literary feature to other literary features in the extract.**

---

## Literary Feature 3:

---

**Describe a literary feature in the extract.**

**Provide specific examples from the extract.**

**Describe the effect this literary feature has on the reader/audience.**

**Outline links of this literary feature to other literary features in the extract.**

# Activity 8: Analyzing Exam Questions

**Assessment Criteria:** Logical coherence; concise use of language; response to demands of question

**Description:**

- Choose an examination question from the following list. Identify works to which the question will be addressed.

- Identify and highlight the major concepts in the question. These are the words that you think are the most important; the essence of the question.

- Take these words and add some qualifying information showing how these words connect to the chosen works.

- Use these groups of words in your introductory paragraph.

- The words should also appear consistently throughout the rest of your response.

*Remember that exam questions present you with a wide range of possible aspects that you could use as ideas to pursue in other types of assignments such as oral commentaries. Over time this activity will provide you with a bank of ideas to use when analyzing literature.*

## Drama

"To succeed in creating a convincing character, the dramatist needs to give the audience a sense that characters have inner thoughts and feelings." To what extent, and in what ways, does this statement apply to **two** or **three** plays you have studied?

## Poetry

"A good poem is not merely a collection of poetic devices but the expression, through such devices, of underlying ideas." With reference to **at least two** poets you have studied, discuss the ways in which poetic devices are used to support the poets' ideas.

## Prose: The Novel and Short Story

"The art of the storyteller is to hold the attention of the reader." With reference to **two** or **three** works you have studied, discuss ways in which the writers have employed techniques that hold your attention.

## Prose: Other than the Novel or Short Story

With reference to **two** or **three** works you have studied, discuss techniques authors have used to persuade readers to sympathize with their ideas.

## General Questions on Literature

Some writers present a world view that is pessimistic and disorderly, while others present a world of hope and possibility. How, and to what extent, do your writers reflect these views in **two** or **three** works you have studied?

"It is the role of literature to challenge and confront the conventional values of a society." In what ways, and to what extent, have conventional values been challenged in **two** or **three** works you have studied?

(IB, 2007, May Paper 2, TZ0)

**Highlight the question that you have selected from the list above. In the space below write the words that you have chosen from that question; the essence of the question.**

**Write down your thoughts regarding how these words relate to the work/s that you will be addressing.**

**Based on these thoughts add some qualifying information to the words to show how they connect to the chosen works.**

**Write an introductory paragraph with these words appearing multiple times. Remember that you chose them because they were the essence of the question.**

# Text Twelve:

**Assessment Criteria:** meaningful and perceptive linking of works / thorough knowledge and understanding of the content of the extract or works

**Description:** Before you start the course you already have a bank of knowledge that will help you to understand the texts. There may also be some misunderstandings that need clearing up.

- Write down notes regarding what you know about the text, author, time period, language or geographic region.

- In pairs share your own information and include new pieces of information from your partner in your workbook.

- During the course when you begin to look at a text as a class bring all your ideas together on the board to both share ideas and dispel misunderstandings.

## Text 12

**Title:**

**Author:**

**Dates:**

**Country and language of original publication:**

**What do you know about this text, author, time period, language, geographic region or political situation that may be relevant?**

## Activity 2: Quote Bank

**Assessment Criteria:** detailed and persuasive references to the works
**Description:**

- Choose a direct reference from a character in your text. In the case of poetry choose a specific line.

- Comment on the relevance of the reference – what it tells us about the character / poem.

- Finally, comment on the links between these references in terms of their significance for the text as a whole.

---

## Text:

---

**Character One:**

Quote / Reference 1:

Significance:

Quote / Reference 2:

Significance:

Quote / Reference 3:

Significance:

**Comment on the links between these quotes:**

---

## Text:

---

**Character Two:**

Quote / Reference 1:

Significance:

Quote / Reference 2:

Significance:

Quote / Reference 3:

Significance:

**Comment on the links between these quotes:**

## Activity 3: Quote Builder

**Assessment Criteria:** ideas are convincing and show independence of thought

**Description:** Break into small groups or pairs. In turn each group or pair presents a short quote from the text to the opposing team.

The opposing team must supply three pieces of information after hearing the quote:

- Which character the quote is from
- The context in which it appeared in the text
- The significance of the quote for the overall text

The first two have definite answers although the last will be dependent on individual interpretations. All answers that can be justified are acceptable – the language used in the justification of the response is an important aspect of this activity.

## Quote Builder: Round 1 Notes

**Our Quote** (Write it here so you can read it out to the opposition)

**Character:**

**Context:**

**Significance:**

**Opposition Quote** (Just a few notes as you listen to it read out by the opposition)

**Character:**

**Context:**

**Significance:**

## Quote Builder: Round 2 Notes

**Our Quote** (Write it here so you can read it out to the opposition)

**Character:**

**Context:**

**Significance:**

**Opposition Quote** (Just a few notes as you listen to it read out by the opposition)

**Character:**

**Context:**

**Significance:**

## Activity 4: Literary Feature Analysis

**Assessment Criteria:** *critical analysis of the effects of the literary features of the works consistently well illustrated by persuasive examples*
**Description:**

- Copy a passage from your text into one of the spaces below.

- Identify a literary feature and comment on this feature in the 'Literary features' table.

## Copy or paste a short passage from your text here

---
## Literary Feature 1:
---

- Describe a literary feature that you can see in the passage above.


- Provide specific examples from the text.


- Describe the effect this literary feature has on the reader/audience.


- Outline links of this literary feature to others.


---
## Literary Feature 2:
---

- Describe a literary feature that you can see in the passage above.


- Provide specific examples from the text.


- Describe the effect this literary feature has on the reader/audience.


- Outline links of this literary feature to others.

## Literary Feature 3:

- Describe a literary feature that you can see in the passage above.


- Provide specific examples from the text.


- Describe the effect this literary feature has on the reader/audience.


- Outline links of this literary feature to others.


## Literary Feature 4:

- Describe a literary feature that you can see in the passage above.


- Provide specific examples from the text.


- Describe the effect this literary feature has on the reader/audience.


- Outline links of this literary feature to others.

## Activity 5: Shared Reading Response

**Assessment Criteria:** meaningful and perceptive linking of works
**Description:**

- In small groups students take turns speaking about the last thing that you read - generally the current work.

- The listener is required to ask questions as they go along using the following prompt.

- Both the listener and the speaker need to make note of any questions asked at the end of the activity

**Prompt to assist with questioning**

**As the listener you are required to ask questions related to any of the following:**

- **The speaker's knowledge of the content**

- **How parts of the work relate to the work as a whole and to other works?**

- **What effects literary features have on the reader's response?**

*As a listener you need to help the speaker stay focused and to support their ideas with specific references from the work. Your questioning can help them to do this. The speaker needs to use accurate, clear and precise language. By seeking clarification of points you can help the speaker to do this.*

**Shared Reading Response: Record Sheet for questions asked and responses**

## The speaker's knowledge of the content

## How parts of the work relate to the work as a whole and to other works?

## What effects literary features have on the reader's response?

## Other questions

## Activity 6: Connecting Theme and Literary Features in a Text

**Assessment Criteria:** in-depth knowledge of, and very good insight into, aspects of the work / purposeful and effective structure / supporting examples are well integrated

**Description:**

- Identify an idea, or theme, expressed through the text you are analyzing.

- Select up to three literary features that appear in the work that in some way support or are related to that identified idea or theme. Highlight these literary features from the given list. Definitions appear in the Vocabulary Log.

- Explain how the chosen literary features support this idea, or theme in the sections below.

- When completing the sections you should attempt to make links between the literary features in terms of how they support each other in the text.

---

## Text:

---

**Theme/Ideas expressed through a text:**

**Literary features identified:**
Allegory, Alliteration, Allusion, Antagonist, Aside, Association, Assonance, Atmosphere, Audience, Blank Verse, Caesura, Caricature, Characterization, Climax, Connotation, Denotation, Denouement, Dialogue, Diction, Enjambment, Euphemism, Flashback, Foreshadowing, Form, Framed Narrative, Free Verse, Genre, Hyperbole, Imagery, Irony, Metaphor, Meter, Metonymy, Mood, Motif, Myth, Narrator, Occasion, Onomatopoeia, Paradox, Parody, Persona, Personification, Plot, Point of View, Protagonist, Repetition, Rhyme, Satire, Setting, Simile, Soliloquy, Sound, Speaker, Structure, Style, Subplot, Subtext, Symbol, Syntax (sentence structure), Theme, Tone

## Literary Feature 1:

**Describe a literary feature that you can identify in your text.**

**Provide specific examples from the text.**

**Describe the effect this literary feature has on the reader/audience.**

**Outline links of this literary feature to other literary features.**

## Literary Feature 2:

**Describe a literary feature that you can identify in your text.**

**Provide specific examples from the text.**

**Describe the effect this literary feature has on the reader/audience.**

**Outline links of this literary feature to other literary features.**

## Literary Feature 3:

**Describe a literary feature that you can identify in your text.**

**Provide specific examples from the text.**

**Describe the effect this literary feature has on the reader/audience.**

**Outline links of this literary feature to other literary features.**

## Activity 7: Connecting Theme and Literary Features in a Text (Unseen)

**Assessment Criteria:** perceptive understanding of the thought and feeling expressed in the text as well as some of the subtleties of the text / detailed and persuasive references to the text / supporting examples are well integrated / in-depth knowledge of, and very good insight into, aspects of the work / purposeful and effective structure

**Description:** The instructions below are the same as for Activity 6 – you just need to repeat the process for this extract although you may not know the context within which this extract appears. The procedure is exactly the same.

- Identify an idea, or theme, expressed through the text.

- Select an important aspect of the text which supports this theme. Circle this word.

- Identify two literary features that support this aspect of the text. Circle these words.

- Explain how the chosen aspect of the text supports this theme.

- Explain how the chosen literary features support this aspect of the text.

- When you have completed these sections write it all out in one paragraph trying to make the connections as clear as possible.

### Sample extract 12: Margaret Atwood, *Oryx and Crake*

Snowman wakes before dawn. He lies unmoving, listening to the tide coming in, wave after wave sloshing over the various barricades, wish-wash, wish-wash, the rhythm of heartbeat. He would so like to believe he is still asleep.

On the eastern horizon there's a greyish haze, lit now with a rosy, deadly glow. Strange how that colour still seems tender. The offshore towers stand out in dark silhouette against it, rising improbably out of the pink and pale blue of the lagoon. The shrieks of the birds that nest out there and the distant ocean grinding against the ersatz reefs of rusted car parts and jumbled bricks and assorted rubble sound almost like holiday traffic.

Out of habit he looks at his watch - stainless-steel case, burnished aluminum band, still shiny although it no longer works. He wears it now as his only talisman. A blank face is what it shows him: zero hour. It causes a jolt of terror to run through him, this absence of official time. Nobody nowhere knows what time it is.

"Calm down," he tells himself. He takes a few deep breaths, then scratches his bug bites, around but not on the itchiest places, taking care not to knock off any scabs: blood poisoning is the last thing he needs. Then he scans the ground below for wildlife: all quiet, no scales and tails. Left hand, right foot, right hand, left foot, he makes his way down from the tree. After brushing off the twigs and bark, he winds his dirty bedsheet around himself like a toga. He's hung his authentic-replica Red Sox baseball cap on a branch overnight for safekeeping; he checks inside it, flicks out a spider, puts it on.

He walks a couple of yards to the left, pisses into the bushes. "Heads up," he says to the grasshoppers that whir away at the impact. Then he goes to the other side of the tree, well away from his customary urinal, and rummages around in the cache he's improvised from a few slabs of concrete, lining it with wire mesh to keep out the rats and mice. He's stashed some mangoes there, knotted in a plastic bag, and a can of Sveltana No-Meat Cocktail Sausages, and a precious half-bottle of Scotch - no, more like a third - and a chocolate-flavoured energy bar scrounged from a trailer park, limp and sticky inside its foil. He can't bring himself to eat it yet: it might be the last one he'll ever find. He keeps a can opener there too, and for no particular reason an ice pick; and six empty beer bottles, for sentimental reasons and for storing fresh water. Also his sunglasses; he puts them on. One lens is missing but they're better than nothing.

He undoes the plastic bag: there's only a single mango left. Funny, he remembered more. The ants have got in, even though he tied the bag as tightly as he could. Already they're running up his arms, the black kind and the vicious little yellow kind. Surprising what a sharp sting they can give, especially the yellow ones. He rubs them away.

"It is the strict adherence to daily routine that tends towards the maintenance of good morale and the preservation of sanity," he says out loud. He has the feeling he's quoting from a book, some obsolete, ponderous directive written in aid of European colonials running plantations of one kind or another. He can't recall ever having read such a thing, but that means nothing. There are a lot of blank spaces in his stub of a brain, where memory used to be. Rubber plantations, coffee plantations, jute plantations. (What was jute?) They would have been told to wear solar topis, dress for dinner, refrain from raping the natives. It wouldn't have said raping. Refrain from fraternizing with the female inhabitants. Or, put some other way . . .

He bets they didn't refrain, though. Nine times out of ten.

"In view of the mitigating," he says. He finds himself standing with his mouth open, trying to remember the rest of the sentence. He sits down on the ground and begins to eat the mango.

(Atwood, 2003)

---

# Text:

---

**Theme/Ideas expressed through this extract:**

**Literary features identified:**

Allegory, Alliteration, Allusion, Antagonist, Aside, Association, Assonance, Atmosphere, Audience, Blank Verse, Caesura, Caricature, Characterization, Climax, Connotation, Denotation, Denouement, Dialogue, Diction, Enjambment, Euphemism, Flashback, Foreshadowing, Form, Framed Narrative, Free Verse, Genre, Hyperbole, Imagery, Irony, Metaphor, Meter, Metonymy, Mood, Motif, Myth, Narrator, Occasion, Onomatopoeia, Paradox, Parody, Persona, Personification, Plot, Point of View, Protagonist, Repetition, Rhyme, Satire, Setting, Simile, Soliloquy, Sound, Speaker, Structure, Style, Subplot, Subtext, Symbol, Syntax (sentence structure), Theme, Tone

## Literary Feature 1:

**Describe a literary feature in the extract.**

**Provide specific examples from the extract.**

**Describe the effect this literary feature has on the reader/audience.**

**Outline links of this literary feature to other literary features in the extract.**

## Literary Feature 2:

**Describe a literary feature in the extract.**

**Provide specific examples from the extract.**

**Describe the effect this literary feature has on the reader/audience.**

**Outline links of this literary feature to other literary features in the extract.**

## Literary Feature 3:

**Describe a literary feature in the extract.**

**Provide specific examples from the extract.**

**Describe the effect this literary feature has on the reader/audience.**

**Outline links of this literary feature to other literary features in the extract.**

# Activity 8: Analyzing Exam Questions

**Assessment Criteria:** Logical coherence; concise use of language; response to demands of question
**Description:**

- Choose an examination question from the following list. Identify works to which the question will be addressed.

- Identify and highlight the major concepts in the question. These are the words that you think are the most important; the essence of the question.

- Take these words and add some qualifying information showing how these words connect to the chosen works.

- Use these groups of words in your introductory paragraph.

- The words should also appear consistently throughout the rest of your response.

*Remember that exam questions present you with a wide range of possible aspects that you could use as ideas to pursue in other types of assignments such as oral commentaries. Over time this activity will provide you with a bank of ideas to use when analyzing literature.*

## Drama

Setting can often reflect the underlying ideas in a play. In the light of this statement consider the importance and use of setting in **two** or **three** plays you have studied.

## Poetry

"Ambiguity in a poem is perhaps its greatest attraction." Referring closely to poems from **at least two** poets in your study, examine how multiple meanings can be suggested in a poem.

## Prose: The Novel and Short Story

Literature is often about crossing boundaries, both physically and mentally. In what ways, and to what extent, does the crossing of boundaries contribute to **two** or **three** works you have studied?

## Prose: Other than the Novel or Short Story

Authors often write about food and rituals of eating. Discuss **two** or **three** works you have studied in the light of this statement.

## General Questions on Literature

"Memory feeds imagination." To what effect has memory been used in **two** or **three** works you have studied?

"It is impossible for literature to be completely objective." How, and to what extent, does this statement apply to **two** or **three** works you have studied?

(IB, 2007, May Paper 2, TZ0)

**Highlight the question that you have selected from the list above. In the space below write the words that you have chosen from that question; the essence of the question.**

**Write down your thoughts regarding how these words relate to the work/s that you will be addressing.**

**Based on these thoughts add some qualifying information to the words to show how they connect to the chosen works.**

**Write an introductory paragraph with these words appearing multiple times. Remember that you chose them because they were the essence of the question.**

*Text Thirteen:*

**Assessment Criteria:** meaningful and perceptive linking of works / thorough knowledge and understanding of the content of the extract or works

**Description:** Before you start the course you already have a bank of knowledge that will help you to understand the texts. There may also be some misunderstandings that need clearing up.

- Write down notes regarding what you know about the text, author, time period, language or geographic region.

- In pairs share your own information and include new pieces of information from your partner in your workbook.

- During the course when you begin to look at a text as a class bring all your ideas together on the board to both share ideas and dispel misunderstandings.

## Text 13

**Title:**

**Author:**

**Dates:**

**Country and language of original publication:**

**What do you know about this text, author, time period, language, geographic region or political situation that may be relevant?**

## Activity 2: Quote Bank

**Assessment Criteria:** detailed and persuasive references to the works
**Description:**

- Choose a direct reference from a character in your text. In the case of poetry choose a specific line.

- Comment on the relevance of the reference – what it tells us about the character / poem.

- Finally, comment on the links between these references in terms of their significance for the text as a whole.

---

# Text:

---

**Character One:**

Quote / Reference 1:

Significance:

Quote / Reference 2:

Significance:

Quote / Reference 3:

Significance:

**Comment on the links between these quotes:**

## Text:

**Character Two:**

Quote / Reference 1:

Significance:

Quote / Reference 2:

Significance:

Quote / Reference 3:

Significance:

**Comment on the links between these quotes:**

# Activity 3: Quote Builder

**Assessment Criteria:** ideas are convincing and show independence of thought
**Description:** Break into small groups or pairs. In turn each group or pair presents a short quote from the text to the opposing team.
The opposing team must supply three pieces of information after hearing the quote:

- Which character the quote is from
- The context in which it appeared in the text
- The significance of the quote for the overall text

The first two have definite answers although the last will be dependent on individual interpretations. All answers that can be justified are acceptable – the language used in the justification of the response is an important aspect of this activity.

## Quote Builder: Round 1 Notes

**Our Quote** (Write it here so you can read it out to the opposition)

**Character:**

**Context:**

**Significance:**

**Opposition Quote** (Just a few notes as you listen to it read out by the opposition)

**Character:**

**Context:**

**Significance:**

# Quote Builder: Round 2 Notes

**Our Quote** (Write it here so you can read it out to the opposition)

**Character:**

**Context:**

**Significance:**

**Opposition Quote** (Just a few notes as you listen to it read out by the opposition)

**Character:**

**Context:**

**Significance:**

## Activity 4: Literary Feature Analysis

**Assessment Criteria:** *critical analysis of the effects of the literary features of the works consistently well illustrated by persuasive examples*
**Description:**

- Copy a passage from your text into one of the spaces below.

- Identify a literary feature and comment on this feature in the 'Literary features' table.

---

### Copy or paste a short passage from your text here

---

## Literary Feature 1:

- Describe a literary feature that you can see in the passage above.


- Provide specific examples from the text.


- Describe the effect this literary feature has on the reader/audience.


- Outline links of this literary feature to others.


## Literary Feature 2:

- Describe a literary feature that you can see in the passage above.


- Provide specific examples from the text.


- Describe the effect this literary feature has on the reader/audience.


- Outline links of this literary feature to others.

---

## Literary Feature 3:

---

- Describe a literary feature that you can see in the passage above.


- Provide specific examples from the text.


- Describe the effect this literary feature has on the reader/audience.


- Outline links of this literary feature to others.

---

## Literary Feature 4:

---

- Describe a literary feature that you can see in the passage above.


- Provide specific examples from the text.


- Describe the effect this literary feature has on the reader/audience.


- Outline links of this literary feature to others.

# Activity 5: Shared Reading Response

**Assessment Criteria:** meaningful and perceptive linking of works
**Description:**

- In small groups students take turns speaking about the last thing that you read - generally the current work.

- The listener is required to ask questions as they go along using the following prompt.

- Both the listener and the speaker need to make note of any questions asked at the end of the activity

**Prompt to assist with questioning**

**As the listener you are required to ask questions related to any of the following:**


- **The speaker's knowledge of the content**


- **How parts of the work relate to the work as a whole and to other works?**


- **What effects literary features have on the reader's response?**

*As a listener you need to help the speaker stay focused and to support their ideas with specific references from the work. Your questioning can help them to do this. The speaker needs to use accurate, clear and precise language. By seeking clarification of points you can help the speaker to do this.*

**Shared Reading Response: Record Sheet for questions asked and responses**

## The speaker's knowledge of the content

## How parts of the work relate to the work as a whole and to other works?

## What effects literary features have on the reader's response?

## Other questions

## Activity 6: Connecting Theme and Literary Features in a Text

**Assessment Criteria:** in-depth knowledge of, and very good insight into, aspects of the work / purposeful and effective structure / supporting examples are well integrated
**Description:**

- Identify an idea, or theme, expressed through the text you are analyzing.

- Select up to three literary features that appear in the work that in some way support or are related to that identified idea or theme. Highlight these literary features from the given list. Definitions appear in the Vocabulary Log.

- Explain how the chosen literary features support this idea, or theme in the sections below.

- When completing the sections you should attempt to make links between the literary features in terms of how they support each other in the text.

## Text:

**Theme/Ideas expressed through a text:**

**Literary features identified:**
Allegory, Alliteration, Allusion, Antagonist, Aside, Association, Assonance, Atmosphere, Audience, Blank Verse, Caesura, Caricature, Characterization, Climax, Connotation, Denotation, Denouement, Dialogue, Diction, Enjambment, Euphemism, Flashback, Foreshadowing, Form, Framed Narrative, Free Verse, Genre, Hyperbole, Imagery, Irony, Metaphor, Meter, Metonymy, Mood, Motif, Myth, Narrator, Occasion, Onomatopoeia, Paradox, Parody, Persona, Personification, Plot, Point of View, Protagonist, Repetition, Rhyme, Satire, Setting, Simile, Soliloquy, Sound, Speaker, Structure, Style, Subplot, Subtext, Symbol, Syntax (sentence structure), Theme, Tone

## Literary Feature 1:

**Describe a literary feature that you can identify in your text.**

**Provide specific examples from the text.**

**Describe the effect this literary feature has on the reader/audience.**

**Outline links of this literary feature to other literary features.**

## Literary Feature 2:

**Describe a literary feature that you can identify in your text.**

**Provide specific examples from the text.**

**Describe the effect this literary feature has on the reader/audience.**

**Outline links of this literary feature to other literary features.**

## Literary Feature 3:

**Describe a literary feature that you can identify in your text.**

**Provide specific examples from the text.**

**Describe the effect this literary feature has on the reader/audience.**

**Outline links of this literary feature to other literary features.**

# Activity 7: Connecting Theme and Literary Features in a Text (Unseen)

**Assessment Criteria:** perceptive understanding of the thought and feeling expressed in the text as well as some of the subtleties of the text / detailed and persuasive references to the text / supporting examples are well integrated / in-depth knowledge of, and very good insight into, aspects of the work / purposeful and effective structure

**Description:** The instructions below are the same as for Activity 6 – you just need to repeat the process for this extract although you may not know the context within which this extract appears. The procedure is exactly the same.

- Identify an idea, or theme, expressed through the text.

- Select an important aspect of the text which supports this theme. Circle this word.

- Identify two literary features that support this aspect of the text. Circle these words.

- Explain how the chosen aspect of the text supports this theme.

- Explain how the chosen literary features support this aspect of the text.

- When you have completed these sections write it all out in one paragraph trying to make the connections as clear as possible.

### Sample extract 13: Oscar Wilde, *The Importance of Being Earnest*

## ALGERNON

Literary criticism is not your forte, my dear fellow. Don't try it. You should leave that to people who haven't been at a University. They do it so well in the daily papers. What you really are is a Bunburyist. I was quite right in saying you were a Bunburyist. You are one of the most advanced Bunburyists I know.

## JACK

What on earth do you mean?

## ALGERNON

You have invented a very useful younger brother called Ernest, in order that you may be able to come up to town as often as you like. I have invented an invaluable permanent invalid called Bunbury, in order that I may be able to go down into the country whenever I choose. Bunbury is perfectly invaluable. If it wasn't for Bunbury's extraordinary bad health, for instance, I wouldn't be able to dine with you at Willis's to-night, for I have been really engaged to Aunt Augusta for more than a week.

## JACK

I haven't asked you to dine with me anywhere to-night.

## ALGERNON

I know. You are absurdly careless about sending out invitations. It is very foolish of you. Nothing annoys people so much as not receiving invitations.

## JACK

You had much better dine with your Aunt Augusta.

## ALGERNON

I haven't the smallest intention of doing anything of the kind. To begin with, I dined there on Monday, and once a week is quite enough to dine with one's own relations. In the second place, whenever I do dine there I am always treated as a member of the family, and sent down with either no woman at all, or two. In the third place, I know perfectly well whom she will place me next to, to-night. She will place me next Mary Farquhar, who always flirts with her own husband across the dinner-table. That is not very pleasant. Indeed, it is not even decent . . . and that sort of thing is enormously on the increase. The amount of women in London who flirt with their own husbands is perfectly scandalous. It looks so bad. It in simply washing one's clean linen in public. Besides, now that I know you to be a confirmed Bunburyist I naturally want to talk to you about Bunburying. I want to tell you the rules.

## JACK

I'm not a Bunburyist at all. If Gwendolen accepts me, I am going to kill my brother, indeed I think I'll kill him in any case. Cecily is a little too much interested in him. It is rather a bore. So I am going to get rid of Ernest. And I strongly advise you to do the same with Mr . . . with your invalid friend who has the absurd name.

## ALGERNON

Nothing will induce me to part with Bunbury, and if you ever get married, which seems to me extremely problematic, you will be very glad to know Bunbury. A man who marries without knowing Bunbury has a very tedious time of it.

## JACK

That is nonsense. If I marry a charming girl like Gwendolen, and she is the only girl I ever saw in my life that I would marry, I certainly won't want to know Bunbury.

## ALGERNON

Then your wife will. You don't seem to realise, that in married life three is company and two is none.

## JACK

[Sententiously.] That, my dear young friend, is the theory that the corrupt French Drama has been propounding for the last fifty years.

## ALGERNON

Yes; and that the happy English home has proved in half the time.

## JACK

For heaven's sake, don't try to be cynical. It's perfectly easy to be cynical.

## ALGERNON

My dear fellow, it isn't easy to be anything nowadays. There's such a lot of beastly competition about. [The sound of an electric bell is heard.] Ah! that must be Aunt Augusta. Only relatives, or creditors, ever ring in that Wagnerian manner. Now, if I get her out of the way for ten minutes, so that you can have an opportunity for proposing to Gwendolen, may I dine with you to- night at Willis's?

## JACK

I suppose so, if you want to.

## ALGERNON

Yes, but you must be serious about it. I hate people who are not serious about meals. It is so shallow of them.

(Wilde, 2005; originally published 1895)

---

# Text:

---

## Theme/Ideas expressed through this extract:



## Literary features identified:

Allegory, Alliteration, Allusion, Antagonist, Aside, Association, Assonance, Atmosphere, Audience, Blank Verse, Caesura, Caricature, Characterization, Climax, Connotation, Denotation, Denouement, Dialogue, Diction, Enjambment, Euphemism, Flashback, Foreshadowing, Form, Framed Narrative, Free Verse, Genre, Hyperbole, Imagery, Irony, Metaphor, Meter, Metonymy, Mood, Motif, Myth, Narrator, Occasion, Onomatopoeia, Paradox, Parody, Persona, Personification, Plot, Point of View, Protagonist, Repetition, Rhyme, Satire, Setting, Simile, Soliloquy, Sound, Speaker, Structure, Style, Subplot, Subtext, Symbol, Syntax (sentence structure), Theme, Tone

## Literary Feature 1:

**Describe a literary feature in the extract.**

**Provide specific examples from the extract.**

**Describe the effect this literary feature has on the reader/audience.**

**Outline links of this literary feature to other literary features in the extract.**

## Literary Feature 2:

**Describe a literary feature in the extract.**

**Provide specific examples from the extract.**

**Describe the effect this literary feature has on the reader/audience.**

**Outline links of this literary feature to other literary features in the extract.**

## Literary Feature 3:

**Describe a literary feature in the extract.**

**Provide specific examples from the extract.**

**Describe the effect this literary feature has on the reader/audience.**

**Outline links of this literary feature to other literary features in the extract.**

## Activity 7: Connecting Theme and Literary Features in a Text (Unseen)

**Assessment Criteria:** perceptive understanding of the thought and feeling expressed in the text as well as some of the subtleties of the text / detailed and persuasive references to the text / supporting examples are well integrated / in-depth knowledge of, and very good insight into, aspects of the work / purposeful and effective structure

**Description:** The instructions below are the same as for Activity 6 – you just need to repeat the process for this extract although you may not know the context within which this extract appears. The procedure is exactly the same.

- Identify an idea, or theme, expressed through the text.

- Select an important aspect of the text which supports this theme. Circle this word.

- Identify two literary features that support this aspect of the text. Circle these words.

- Explain how the chosen aspect of the text supports this theme.

- Explain how the chosen literary features support this aspect of the text.

- When you have completed these sections write it all out in one paragraph trying to make the connections as clear as possible.

### Sample extract 14: Toni Morrison, *Beloved*

124 was spiteful. Full of a baby's venom. The women in the house knew it and so did the children. For years each put up with the spite in his own way, but in 1873 Sethe and her daughter Denver were its only victims. The Grandmother, Baby Suggs, was dead, and the sons, Howard and Buglar, had run away by the time they were thirteen years old – as soon as merely looking in a mirror shattered it (that was the signal for Buglar); as soon as two tiny hand prints appeared in the cake (that was it for Howard). Neither boy waited to see more; another kettleful of chickpeas smoking in a heap on the floor; soda crackers crumbled and strewn in a line next to the doorsill. Nor did they wait for one of the relief periods: the weeks, months even, when nothing was disturbed. No. Each fled at once – the moment the house committed what was for him the one insult not to be borne or witnessed a second time. Within two months, in the dead of winter, leaving the grandmother, Baby Suggs; Sethe, their mother; and their little sister, Denver, all by themselves in the gray and white house in Bluestone Road. It didn't have a number then, because Cincinnati didn't stretch that far. In fact, Ohio had been calling itself a state only seventy years when first one brother and then the next stuffed quilt packing into his hat, snatched up his shoes, and crept away from the lively spite the house felt for them.

Baby Suggs didn't even raise her head. From her sickbed she heard them go but that wasn't the reason she lay still. It was a wonder to her that her grandsons had taken so long to realize that every house wasn't like the one on Bluestone Road. Suspended between the nastiness of life and the meanness of the dead, she couldn't get interested in leaving life or living it, let alone the fright of two creeping-off boys. Her past had been like her present – intolerable – and since she knew death was anything but forgetfulness, she used the little energy left her for pondering color.

"Bring a little lavender in, if you got any. Pink if you don't."

And Seth would oblige her with anything from fabric to her own tongue. Winter in Ohio was especially rough if you had any appetite for color. Sky provided the only drama, and counting on a Cincinnati horizon for life's principal joy was reckless indeed. So Seth and the girl Denver did what they could, and what the house permitted, for her. Together they waged a perfunctory battle against the outrageous behavior of that place; against turned-over slop jars, smacks on the behind, and gusts of foul air. For they understood the source of the outrage as well as they knew the source of light.

Baby Suggs died shortly after the brothers left, with no interest whatsoever in their leave taking or hers, and right afterward Seth and Denver decided to end the persecution by calling forth the ghost that tried them so. Perhaps a conversation, they thought, an exchange of views or something would help. So they held hands and said, "Come on. Come on. You may as well just come on."

The sideboard took a step forward but nothing else did.

"Grandma Baby must be stopping it," said Denver. She was ten and still mad at Baby Suggs for dying.

Sethe opened her eyes. "I doubt that," she said.

"Then why don't it come?"

"You forgetting how little it is," said her mother. "She wasn't even two years old when she died.

Too little to understand. Too little to talk much even.

"Maybe she don't want to understand," said Denver.

"Maybe. But if she'd only come, I could make it clear to her." Sethe released her daughter's hand and together they pushed the sideboard back against the wall. Outside a driver whipped his horse into the gallop local people felt necessary when they passed 124.

"For a baby she throws a powerful spell," said Denver.

"No more powerful than the way I loved her," Sethe answered and there it was again.

(Morrison, 1987)

---

# Text:

---

**Theme/Ideas expressed through this extract:**


**Literary features identified:**

Allegory, Alliteration, Allusion, Antagonist, Aside, Association, Assonance, Atmosphere, Audience, Blank Verse, Caesura, Caricature, Characterization, Climax, Connotation, Denotation, Denouement, Dialogue, Diction, Enjambment, Euphemism, Flashback, Foreshadowing, Form, Framed Narrative, Free Verse, Genre, Hyperbole, Imagery, Irony, Metaphor, Meter, Metonymy, Mood, Motif, Myth, Narrator, Occasion, Onomatopoeia, Paradox, Parody, Persona, Personification, Plot, Point of View, Protagonist, Repetition, Rhyme, Satire, Setting, Simile, Soliloquy, Sound, Speaker, Structure, Style, Subplot, Subtext, Symbol, Syntax (sentence structure), Theme, Tone

## Literary Feature 1:

**Describe a literary feature in the extract.**

**Provide specific examples from the extract.**

**Describe the effect this literary feature has on the reader/audience.**

**Outline links of this literary feature to other literary features in the extract.**

## Literary Feature 2:

**Describe a literary feature in the extract.**

**Provide specific examples from the extract.**

**Describe the effect this literary feature has on the reader/audience.**

**Outline links of this literary feature to other literary features in the extract.**

## Literary Feature 3:

**Describe a literary feature in the extract.**

**Provide specific examples from the extract.**

**Describe the effect this literary feature has on the reader/audience.**

**Outline links of this literary feature to other literary features in the extract.**

## Activity 7: Connecting Theme and Literary Features in a Text (Unseen)

**Assessment Criteria:** perceptive understanding of the thought and feeling expressed in the text as well as some of the subtleties of the text / detailed and persuasive references to the text / supporting examples are well integrated / in-depth knowledge of, and very good insight into, aspects of the work / purposeful and effective structure

**Description:** The instructions below are the same as for Activity 6 – you just need to repeat the process for this extract although you may not know the context within which this extract appears. The procedure is exactly the same.

- Identify an idea, or theme, expressed through the text.

- Select an important aspect of the text which supports this theme. Circle this word.

- Identify two literary features that support this aspect of the text. Circle these words.

- Explain how the chosen aspect of the text supports this theme.

- Explain how the chosen literary features support this aspect of the text.

- When you have completed these sections write it all out in one paragraph trying to make the connections as clear as possible.

### Sample extract 15: Emily Bronte, *Wuthering Heights*

He threw himself into a chair, laughing and groaning, and bid them all stand off, for he was nearly killed - he would not have such another walk for the three kingdoms. 'And at the end of it to be flighted to death!' he said, opening his great-coat, which he held bundled up in his arms. 'See here, wife! I was never so beaten with anything in my life: but you must e'en take it as a gift of God; though it's as dark almost as if it came from the devil.'

We crowded round, and over Miss Cathy's head I had a peep at a dirty, ragged, black-haired child; big enough both to walk and talk: indeed, its face looked older than Catherine's; yet when it was set on its feet, it only stared round, and repeated over and over again some gibberish that nobody could understand. I was frightened, and Mrs. Earnshaw was ready to fling it out of doors: she did fly up, asking how he could fashion to bring that gypsy brat into the house, when they had their own bairns to feed and fend for? What he meant to do with it, and whether he were mad? The master tried to explain the matter; but he was really half dead with fatigue, and all that I could make out, amongst her scolding, was a tale of his seeing it starving, and houseless, and as good as dumb, in the streets of Liverpool, where he picked it up and inquired for its owner. Not a soul knew to whom it belonged, he said; and his money and time being both limited, he thought it better to take it home with him at once, than run into vain expenses there: because he was determined he would not leave it as he found it. Well, the conclusion was, that my mistress grumbled herself calm; and Mr. Earnshaw told me to wash it, and give it clean things, and let it sleep with the children.

Hindley and Cathy contented themselves with looking and listening till peace was restored: then, both began searching their father's pockets for the presents he had promised them. The former was a boy of fourteen, but when he drew out what had been a fiddle, crushed to morsels in the great-coat, he blubbered aloud; and Cathy, when she learned the master had lost her whip in attending on the stranger, showed her humor by grinning and spitting at the stupid little thing; earning for her pains a sound blow from her father, to teach her cleaner manners. They entirely refused to have it in bed with them, or even in their room; and I had no more sense, so I put it on the landing of the stairs, hoping it might he gone on the morrow. By chance, or else attracted by hearing his voice, it crept to Mr. Earnshaw's door, and there he found it on quitting his chamber. Inquiries were made as to how it got there; I was obliged to confess, and in recompense for my cowardice and inhumanity was sent out of the house.

This was Heathcliff's first introduction to the family. On coming back a few days afterwards (for I did not consider my banishment perpetual), I found they had christened him 'Heathcliff': it was the name of a son who died in childhood, and it has served him ever since, both for Christian and surname. Miss Cathy and he were now very thick; but Hindley hated him: and to say the truth I did the same; and we plagued and went on with him shamefully: for I wasn't reasonable enough to feel my injustice, and the mistress never put in a word on his behalf when she saw him wronged.

He seemed a sullen, patient child; hardened, perhaps, to ill- treatment: he would stand Hindley's blows without winking or shedding a tear, and my pinches moved him only to draw in a breath and open his eyes, as if he had hurt himself by accident, and nobody was to blame. This endurance made old Earnshaw furious, when he discovered his son persecuting the poor fatherless child, as he called him. He took to Heathcliff strangely, believing all he said (for that matter, he said precious little, and generally the truth), and petting him up far above Cathy, who was too mischievous and wayward for a favourite.

So, from the very beginning, he bred bad feeling in the house........

(Bronte, 2002; originally published in 1847)

---

# Text:

---

**Theme/Ideas expressed through this extract:**


**Literary features identified:**

Allegory, Alliteration, Allusion, Antagonist, Aside, Association, Assonance, Atmosphere, Audience, Blank Verse, Caesura, Caricature, Characterization, Climax, Connotation, Denotation, Denouement, Dialogue, Diction, Enjambment, Euphemism, Flashback, Foreshadowing, Form, Framed Narrative, Free Verse, Genre, Hyperbole, Imagery, Irony, Metaphor, Meter, Metonymy, Mood, Motif, Myth, Narrator, Occasion, Onomatopoeia, Paradox, Parody, Persona, Personification, Plot, Point of View, Protagonist, Repetition, Rhyme, Satire, Setting, Simile, Soliloquy, Sound, Speaker, Structure, Style, Subplot, Subtext, Symbol, Syntax (sentence structure), Theme, Tone

## Literary Feature 1:

**Describe a literary feature in the extract.**

**Provide specific examples from the extract.**

**Describe the effect this literary feature has on the reader/audience.**

**Outline links of this literary feature to other literary features in the extract.**

## Literary Feature 2:

**Describe a literary feature in the extract.**

**Provide specific examples from the extract.**

**Describe the effect this literary feature has on the reader/audience.**

**Outline links of this literary feature to other literary features in the extract.**

## Literary Feature 3:

**Describe a literary feature in the extract.**

**Provide specific examples from the extract.**

**Describe the effect this literary feature has on the reader/audience.**

**Outline links of this literary feature to other literary features in the extract.**

## Activity 8: Analyzing Exam Questions

**Assessment Criteria:** logical coherence, concise use of language, response to demands of question

**Description:**

- Choose an examination question from the following list. Identify works to which the question will be addressed.

- Identify and highlight the major concepts in the question. These are the words that you think are the most important; the essence of the question.

- Take these words and add some qualifying information based on your thoughts regarding the application of this question to specific works.

- Use these groups of words in your introductory paragraph.

- The words should also appear consistently throughout the rest of your response of your essay.

Remember that exam questions present you with a wide range of possible aspects that you could use as ideas to pursue in other types of assignments such as oral commentaries. This activity will over time provide you with a bank of ideas to use when analyzing literature.

## Drama

"Some plays are either serious or light-hearted; others include both elements."

Consider some of the ways in which either or both sorts of element are presented in two or three plays that you have studied and discuss their importance for the understanding of the plays as a whole.

## Poetry

"Much poetry concerns itself with the impact of change." Explore the ways in which change of various kinds is presented in the poetry you have studied. You must refer closely to the work of two or three poets in your study and base your answer on a total of three or four poems.

## Prose: The Novel and Short Story

How far, and in what ways, do writers present issues of self-awareness and/or self-deception in two or three novels or short stories you have studied?

## Prose other than the Novel and Short Story

Compare the ways in which the relations between the writer and his community are presented in two or three works you have studied.

## General Questions on Literature

Using two or three of the works you have studied, discuss how and to what extent the writers have shown the pervasive influence of the past.

If one of the roles of literature is to provide insight into human nature, by what techniques and to what degree did your texts offer you such insight? Discuss with reference to two or three works you have studied.

(IB, 2005 HL Paper 2, TZ0)

Highlight the question that you have selected from the list above. In the space below write the words that you have chosen from that question; the essence of the question.

Write down your thoughts regarding how these words relate to the work/s that you will be addressing.

Based on these thoughts add some qualifying information to the words to show how they connect to the chosen works.

Write an introductory paragraph with these words appearing multiple times. Remember that you chose them because they were the essence of the question.

# Vocabulary Log

## Final Activity : Vocabulary Log

**Assessment Criteria:** *precise use of wide vocabulary*
**Description:**
Keeping a log of vocabulary relevant to the study of literature and examples related to each of the texts that are being studied.
For each given word look at the meaning and examples provided and search for other examples from the works studied in your course.

*You will need to keep coming back to this vocabulary list during the course. It is extremely important that you gradually expand the range of vocabulary that you are able to introduce into your written and spoken communication. These words carry very specific meanings and they will allow you to say things concisely and precisely.*

The following definitions have been adapted from *Collins Dictionary: Literary Terms* (Quinn, 2004), *The Penguin Dictionary of Literary Terms and Literary Theory* (Cuddon, 1999), *A Glossary of Literary Terms* (9th Edition) (Abrams & Harpham, 2009) and *Oxford Dictionary of Literary Terms* (Baldick, 2008).

# Allegory

Allegory is an extended metaphor. The extension of the metaphor causes the narrative, the surface story, to carry a parallel, symbolic or metaphorical meaning. An allegory may continue for only part of a text or throughout a whole text.

- In Conrad's *Heart of Darkness* (2002; originally published in 1899) the central part of the unknown African continent is a metaphor for the unknown nature of the human heart. This metaphor is maintained throughout the whole text so the literal journey of Marlow into the heart of the unknown African continent to discover the truth about Kurtz supports a parallel metaphoric journey into the unknown human heart to discover the truth of human nature.

- *An example from a text in your course:*

# Alliteration

Alliteration is the repetition of stressed single sounds, generally consonant sounds, at the beginning of a series of successive words.

- The title of Sylvia Plath's poem 'The Arrival of The Bee Box' (1998) uses the repeated consonant 'b' sounds in '<u>B</u>ee' and '<u>B</u>ox'.

- *An example from a text in your course:*

# Allusion

Allusion is a reference within a text to a person, place, event outside the text, or even to another work of literature or art. A topical allusion is a reference to events well known during the time period of the text. A personal allusion is a reference to a specific individual.

- In James Joyce's Ulysses 'the cracked looking glass of a servant' is a topical allusion to a statement in Oscar Wilde's *Intentions* 'I can quite understand your objection to art being treated as a mirror. You think it would reduce genius to the position of a cracked looking glass.' (Thornton, 1968) As can be seen in this example, the allusion is dependent on the reader or audience sharing a piece of knowledge so that the connection can be made.

- A more obvious personal allusion comes from George Orwell's novel *Animal Farm* (1990; originally published in 1945) where the name of a character is Napoleon, an obvious allusion to Napoleon Bonaparte (1769 - 1821), the connection being made even clearer by shared characteristics beyond the name.

- *An example from a text in your course:*

# Antagonist

The antagonist opposes the main character in drama or fiction. The antagonist is therefore defined in terms of their relationship to the main character, the protagonist.

- The evil Iago as the antagonist opposes Othello, the protagonist, in *Othello* (2004; originally published approximately 1621) by Shakespeare.

- The righteous Macduff as the antagonist opposes Macbeth, the protagonist, in *Macbeth* (2004; originally published in approximately 1603) by Shakespeare.

- The manipulative Lu Kuei as the antagonist opposes his daughter Su Feng, the protagonist, in the play *Thunderstorm* (2001; originally published in Chinese in 1933) by Tsao Yu.

- *An example from a text in your course:*

# Aside

An aside in drama is the direction of brief comments to the audience. The comments are inaudible to the other characters on stage. The aside differs from a soliloquy in that a soliloquy is the expression of thoughts or feelings by a character while alone on stage and in this sense can be described as thinking aloud.

- Othello in Shakespeare's tragic play *Othello* (2004; originally published approximately 1621) addresses the audience after Roderigo has attacked Cassio, using six lines which include the phrases, 'O brave Iago, honest and just,' and later in the aside referring to Desdemona, 'Strumpet I come.' In this case even though the audience is directly addressed by Othello they are powerless to intervene, to stop the terrible events foreshadowed by this aside heightening the tension felt by the audience.

- *An example from a text in your course:*

---

# Association

---

Association is the shared connection between an object and an idea.

- In Albert Camus' *The Stranger* (1989; originally published in French in 1942) the association of a mother's funeral with the emotion of grief is used to set the protagonist, Meursault, apart from the society in which he lives as he does not visibly grieve at his mother's funeral.

- In Joseph Conrad's *Heart of Darkness* (2002; originally published in 1899) the protagonist, Marlow discovers rusted and discarded locomotives which are associated with European civilization. As a result of this association the reader can sense that European civilization is breaking down on the African continent. Through this association the locomotives carry symbolic meaning.

- *An example from a text in your course:*

---

# Assonance

---

Assonance is the repetition of similar vowel sounds in a series of words.

- In the poem 'Byzantium' (Yeats, 1996), originally published in 1928, William Butler Yeats uses the repetition of the combination of 'o' sounds in the last line of this poem, "that dolphin-torn, that gong-tormented sea".

- *An example from a text in your course:*

---

# Atmosphere (mood)

---

Atmosphere is the sense of emotion experienced by the reader or audience. The term is used interchangeably with mood. *Atmosphere/mood*, the sense of emotion experienced by the reader or audience, is heavily influenced by *tone*, the attitude of the speaker (usually the narrator) to the reader or audience. Setting and many other literary features can all produce subtle shifts in atmosphere/mood.

- In Tsao Yu's play *Thunderstorm* (2001; originally published in Chinese in 1933) the atmosphere becomes increasingly claustrophobic as the play progresses. The setting is a large house, close and oppressive with curtains drawn. The overall tone of high drama creates mounting tension through the rising action of the plot and this claustrophobic atmosphere becomes more pronounced as the play progresses. The audience senses or feels that the characters are trapped, literally in the house, but also figuratively in the disintegrating society in which they live. As can be seen in this example atmosphere is the result of a number of other literary features working together.

- *An example from a text in your course:*

# Audience

An audience watches a dramatic performance. A reader reads a written text. This distinction is important when commenting on the effects of literary features in a play. Plays are written to be performed so although plays are often read in a classroom situation it is important to remember when analyzing plays that the audience is a group of people watching the action on stage, not an individual reading the play as a written text.

- Modern audiences respond to elements of Shakespearean plays in a very different manner than the original Elizabethan audiences.

- *An example from a text in your course:*

# Blank Verse

Blank verse is unrhymed iambic pentameter. Iambic pentameter is verse consisting of lines with five iambs, pairs of syllables the first short, the second long. Two famous examples of blank verse are Shakespeare's plays and Milton's *Paradise Lost*.

- Milton used blank verse in *Paradise Lost* (2003; originally published in 1667). This example comes from Book 1:

    The mind is its own place, and in itself

    Can make a heav'n of hell, a hell of heav'n.

- Shakespeare also used blank verse. This example is from *Macbeth* (2004; originally published in approximately 1603) and as you can see, although the lines are shared by two characters the iambic pentameter is not broken:

|   |   |
|---|---|
| *Macbeth:* | If I stand here, I saw him. |
| *Lady Macbeth:* | Fie, for shame! |

- *An example from a text in your course:*

---

# Caesura

---

Caesura is a pause in a line of verse which may be metrical or rhetorical. The pause in not always indicated by punctuation and it often falls in the middle of a line.

- The use of caesura by Plath in the second stanza of her poem 'Blue Moles' (Plath, 1998, p. 49) emphasizes the word 'already' giving the reader the sense of powerlessness over these events which have already come to pass, nothing can now be done:

    Bare no sinister spaces. Already

    The Moles look neutral as the stones.

- *An example from a text in your course:*

---

# Caricature

---

Caricature is an exaggerated description of a character so that a specific trait becomes an overwhelming feature.

- Lady Bracknell in Wild's *The Importance of Being Earnest* (2005; originally published 1895) is an exaggerated description of a member of the upper class and the particular trait that is evident in the following exchange is blissful ignorance which Wilde satirized through this caricature.

|   |   |
|---|---|
| *Lady Bracknell:* | A very good age to be married at. I have always been of the opinion that a man who desires to be married should know either absolutely everything or absolutely nothing. Which do you know? |
| *Jack:* | *(after some hesitation)* I know nothing Lady Bracknell. |
| *Lady Bracknell:* | I am pleased to hear it. I do not approve of anything that tampers with natural ignorance. Ignorance is like a delicate exotic fruit; touch it and the bloom is gone. The whole theory of modern education is unsound. Fortunately in England, at any rate, education produces no effects whatsoever. If it did, it would prove a serious danger to the upper classes… |

- *An example from a text in your course:*

## Characterization

Characterization is the portrayal of a person depicted in drama or prose. The portrayal may include physical, emotional, social and cultural attributes.

- Alice Walker in her novel *The Color Purple* (Walker, 1982) constructed a vulnerable, confused but defiant young girl, Celie, trapped in an incestuous, abusive domestic situation through the use of the protagonist's first person narration in the form of diary entries in the opening chapter:

> Dear God
>
> He act like he can't stand me no more. Say I'm evil an always up to no good. He took my other little baby, a boy this time. But I don't think he kilt it. I think he sold it to a man an his wife over Monticello. I got breasts full of milk running down myself. He say Why don't you look decent? Put on something. But what I'm sposed to put on? I don't have nothing.
>
> I keep hoping he find someone to marry. I see him looking at my sister. She scared. But I say I'll take care of you. With God help.
>
> (Walker, 1982)

It is important to remember that when characterization is examined it is not only the attributes of the character that have to be looked at, but how those attributes are portrayed. For example in the brief passage above you may note that Nellie is, despite her horrific situation, defiant. What is it in the text that leads you to think this?

- *An example from a text in your course:*

## Climax

Climax is the part of a narrative where a resolution to a crisis is reached. Rising action precedes the climax and falling action follows.

- In the play *Thunderstorm* (2001; originally published in Chinese in 1933) by Tsao Yu the climax is reached with the death of Su Feng, her unborn child and Chou Chung, the sins of the parents being paid for with the lives of two out of three children and the unborn grand child. The last remaining son, Chou Ping's subsequent suicide is part of the falling action leaving the older generation distraught and alone. You may have guessed that this play is a tragedy.

- *An* example *from a text in your course:*

---

# Connotation

---

Connotation is an association a word has outside of its literal meaning which has been acquired through use. Denotation is a word's most literal meaning.
- The handshake in Shaw's *Mrs Warren's Profession* (1991; originally published in 1902) when Vivie meets Crofts is literally a formal part of their greeting requested by Crofts. The strength of Vivie's handshake both with Praed and Crofts however carries connotations of independence and defiance.

- *An* example *from a text in your course:*

---

# Denotation

---

Denotation is a word's most literal meaning of a word. A word will also carry connotations which are the associations outside of its literal meaning.
- In George Orwell's novel *1984* (2003; originally published 1949) Winston, the protagonist purchases and writes in a diary. The most literal meaning of diary is a book to write your thoughts in. Obviously in this novel the diary carries significance in terms of its meaning outside of what the word *diary* denotes. The word diary carries significant connotations related to rebellion, independence and truth in *1984*.

- *An* example *from a text in your course:*

# Denouement

Denouement is the action at the end of a narrative, after the climax, when the complications are unraveled.

- The denouement in Shakespeare's tragic play *Othello* (2004; originally published approximately 1621) involves the unmasking of Iago and the realization of Othello that he has murdered an innocent Desdemona. All of the loose ends are tied up with the capture of Iago, the suicide of Othello, Cassio's appointment as Governor and Lodivico's promise to relate events, 'this heavy act with heavy heart relate', to the Venetian State. Justice is served and order is restored during this denouement.

- *An* example *from a text in your course:*

# Dialogue

Dialogue is the speech of characters, generally a verbal exchange between characters.

- In Shusaku Endo's novel *Deep River* (1994; originally published in Japanese in 1993) the characters' dialogue is mixed with narration. It is important to remember the role that the narrator plays in relaying this dialogue and the particular point of view from which it is related:

  > Her wrist had grown decidedly thinner, providing evidence that death was subtly spreading through her body. She responded with her characteristic smile and said, 'You're getting enough to eat aren't you? Take your laundry over to my mother's.'
  > 'Right.'
  > He went out into the corridor. He felt as though chunks of lead had been jammed into his chest. (p. 10)

- *An* example *from a text in your course:*

---

# Diction

---

Diction is the author's choice of words in a text.

- In Toni Morrison's novel *Beloved* (1987) the opening sentences are, '124 was spiteful. Full of a baby's venom.' In terms of diction Morrison's choice of the word 'venom' may suggest to the reader that the origin of the spitefulness in the house at 124 is organic rather than supernatural. The juxtaposition of the terms 'baby' and 'venom' also creates an ambiguity in these opening lines as even though the word 'venom' suggests malevolence the term 'baby' suggests innocence and helplessness. Diction relates to the choice that Morrison made to use this particular word 'venom' instead of the thousands of alternative words available and the effects of this particular choice on the work.

- *An* example *from a text in your course:*

---

# Enjambment

---

Enjambment in verse is the continuation of a sentence from one line or couplet to the next without pause.

- In William Wordsworth's poem 'There was a Boy' (Wordsworth & Gill (Ed.), William Wordsworth: The Major Works, 2008) originally published in 1800, enjambment is used to focus attention on the action 'shout' which falls at the end of the line of verse although the meaning of the sentence is carried over to the next line.

> That they might answer him.--And they would shout
> Across the watery vale, and shout again,

- *An* example *from a text in your course:*

# Euphemism

Euphemism is the substitution of a mild or inoffensive expression for one that is blunt or possibly offensive.

- In George Bernard Shaw's *Mrs Warren's Profession* (1991; originally published in 1902) Crofts, a long term friend and business partner of Vivie's mother, when explaining to Vivie the nature of her mother, Mrs Warren's businesses refers to their brothels as 'the business' a much milder term.

- *An* example *from a text in your course:*

# Flashback

A flashback is a scene that is inserted in a play, novel or poem which shows events which occurred in a previous time period.

- In Tsao Yu's **play** *Thunderstorm* (2001; originally published in Chinese in 1933) a **flashback** is used to identify Lu Ma as Chou Pu-Yuan's former lover and mother of two of his sons. Chou Pu-Yuan, ignorant of Lu Ma's real identity, not having seen her for twenty years, asks her if she knows this person and she relates her own story in the third person only revealing her true identity at the end of the story. This story told by Lu Ma is a type of flashback. As Lu Ma's daughter is pregnant with Chou Pu-Yuan's oldest son's child this flashback introduces a dramatic complication to the plot with ongoing ramifications for all characters.

- *An* example *from a text in your course:*

# Foreshadowing

Foreshadowing is a hint about something that will happen later in the narrative.

- In Conrad's *Heart of Darkness* (2002; originally published in 1899) Marlow, the protagonist foreshadows his journey into a metaphoric hell through his allusion to Dante's *Inferno* (2006; originally published in Italian in the early 1300s ).

> My purpose was to stroll into the shade for a moment; but no sooner within than it seemed to me I had stepped into the gloomy circle of some Inferno. (p. 27)

The fact that Dante's *Inferno* describes a journey through nine circles of hell foreshadows the other circles into which Marlow is doomed to wander during his upriver journey in search for Kurtz.

- *An* example *from a text in your course:*

# Form

Form is the overall design of a work. It is often associated with genre types such as the short story for example which have consistent overall designs. The overall design could also be recognized in the presentation of the ideas in the text such as a 'journey of discovery' or 'coming of age'. The term structure is sometimes used interchangeably with form although structure is generally considered to relate to the internal cohesion of a work, how it fits together, rather than the form, the overall design.

- Shakespeare's plays generally take the form of either a tragedy or a comedy presented in blank verse over five acts.

- Endo Shusaku's novel *Deep River* (1994; originally published in Japanese in 1993) takes the form of a journey of discovery for each of the members of the Japanese tour group visiting the Ganges.

- *An* example *from a text in your course:*

# Framed Narrative

A framed narrative is a story contained within another story. The reliability of narrators may be used to raise questions in framed narratives.

- Emily Bronte's novel *Wuthering Heights* (2002; originally published in 1847) is structured as a framed narrative with Lockwood recounting a story that he has been told by Nellie who also, in her narrative, recounts stories that she has herself been told. In this sense although Lockwood it the main narrator parts of the narrative are presented as stories within stories within stories involving multiple narrators.

- *An* example *from a text in your course:*

---

## Free Verse

---

Free verse has no regular meter or line length and usually does not rhyme.
Walt Whitman's poem 'Ashes of Soldiers' (Whitman, 2004, p. 623) originally published in 1900 is an example of a poem with no regular meter of line length:

> ASHES of soldiers!
> As I muse, retrospective, murmuring a chant in thought,
> Lo! the war resumes—again to my sense your shapes,
> And again the advance of armies.

- *An* example *from a text in your course:*

---

## Genre

---

An identifiable type of film or literature conforming to a set of understood rules governing form and/or content.

- *Mice and Men* (2002;originally published in 1937) by John Steinbeck is defined as a novella in terms of genre as it is shorter than a novel and longer than a short story. The rules for classification in this case relate to length.

- *An* example *from a text in your course:*

---

## Hyperbole

---

Hyperbole is an exaggerated expression.
- Sylvia Plath's poem used hyperbole in 'The Colossus' (1998, p. 20), originally published in 1957, to accentuate the disparity between the speaker and the subject of the poem:

I crawl like an ant in mourning
Over the weedy acres of your brow

- *An* example *from a text in your course:*

---

# Imagery

---

Imagery is the use of language to represent a sense experience. The image portrayed may be literal or figurative. Images can be visual (sight), tactile (touch), auditory (hearing), olfactory (smell), gustatory (taste), kinesthetic (movement) or organic (feelings).

- In Emily Bronte's *Wuthering Heights* (2002; originally published in 1847) the visual imagery associated with the windows of the two properties, Thrushcross Grange with large, open windows and Wuthering Heights with small, sunken inward looking windows allows the reader to sense certain personality traits of the respective inhabitants.

- *An* example *from a text in your course:*

---

# Irony

---

Irony is a sense of incongruity between what is said and what is meant (verbal irony or sarcasm), of an intention and a result or of appearance and reality (situational irony). Related to situational irony, in drama if the audience is aware of something that certain characters on stage are not this sense of incongruity is referred to as dramatic irony.

- In Shaw's *Mrs Warren's Profession* (1991; originally published in 1902) Crofts uses the expression to Vivian, 'On my word as a gentleman I didn't.' Vivie senses the irony of his protest as although he said this sincerely Vivie knows that, although he considers himself so, he is anything but a gentleman and this had become very apparent in their preceding conversation. In this sense the gulf between Croft's intention and the result of his protest in this situation creates a sense of irony. Crofts is unaware of the sense of irony in this situation.

- Also in Shaw's *Mrs Warren's Profession* (1991; originally published in 1902) Frank says very disrespectfully to his father, 'Half-past eleven. Nice hour for a rector to come down to breakfast.' His father replies, 'Don't mock, Frank: don't mock.' Frank of course was saying the opposite to what he meant in this instance of verbal irony. A short exchange like this gives the audience an important insight into the relationship between the father and son.

- In Shakespeare's play *Othello* (2004; originally published approximately 1621) dramatic irony is developed when Othello hides in order to hear a conversation which the manipulative Iago sets up so that although Cassio, Othello's Lieutenant, is speaking of his relationship with his own mistress, Bianca, Othello believes that Cassio is referring to Othello's wife Desdemona – the final proof, or so Othello believes, of their affair. The audience knows that this is not true but yet is powerless to intervene.

- *An* example *from a text in your course:*

# Metaphor

Metaphor involves the one object taking on the attributes of another. The object of the metaphor loses its own identity through this process and in this sense the metaphor is the most powerful form of comparison, much stronger than the simile where only partial qualities are attributed.

- In Joseph Conrad's *Heart of Darkness* (2002; originally published in 1899) Marlowe says, "I shook hands with this miracle," when he meets the Company's chief accountant. The accountant's spotlessly elegant attire is incongruous with the 'shadows of disease and starvation, lying confusedly in the greenish gloom.' As the workers become 'shadows' and the accountant becomes a 'miracle' through the use of these two metaphors it seems to the reader that Marlowe is not quite sure if what he is seeing is real or not. The visual imagery of the 'green gloom' contributes to this effect.

- *An* example *from a text in your course:*

# Meter

Meter refers to the rhythmical pattern in a line of verse. Poetry that does not have a fixed meter is referred to as *free verse*.

- Iambic pentameter is the meter, the rhythmical pattern, of Shakespeare's plays.

- *An* example *from a text in your course:*

---

## Metonym

---

Metonym is the substitution of the name of an attribute of something to represent the whole. This rhetorical strategy allows the writer to describe something indirectly by using words that are closely associated with it.

- The use of the word 'Shakespeare' referring to all of the works of the playwright or the use of the term 'The bench' referring to all of the members of a sporting team waiting on the sideline of a game as potential replacements are examples of metonym. 'The Crown' is also used to refer to a Monarchy.

- *An* example *from a text in your course:*

---

## Mood (atmosphere)

---

Mood is the sense of emotion experienced by the reader or audience. The term is used interchangeably with atmosphere. Atmosphere/mood, the sense of emotion experienced by the reader or audience, is heavily influenced by tone, the attitude of the speaker (usually the narrator) to the reader or audience. Setting and many other literary features can all produce subtle shifts in atmosphere/mood.

- In the opening scene of *Three Sisters* (1990; originally published in Russian in 1901) by Anton Chekhov the mood is nostalgic yet hopeful, generated in part by Irena's wistful tone as she speaks of seemingly realistic and concrete plans to return to Moscow:

    *Irena:*    To go to Moscow. To sell up the house, to finish with everything here, and off to Moscow...

- *An* example *from a text in your course:*

# Motif

Motif is a recurring element in a work. It could be an object, image, symbol, action or idea. Motif is often confused with *theme* which is an idea that pervades a work. A useful way to distinguish *motif* from a *theme* is to consider theme as an abstract idea that pervades a text and motif as a more concrete example of that idea.

- Milk is an important motif in some of Anita Desai's short stories such as 'Studies in the Park' (Desai, 1998):

  Then, worst of all, the milk arrives. In the tallest glass in the house. 'Suno, drink your milk. Good for you, Suno. You need it. Now, before the exams. Must have it, Suno. Drink.' (p. 21)

  I kept them shut so as not to see all the puzzled, pleading, indignant faces of my family around me, but I could not shut out their voices.
  'Suno, Suno,' I heard them croon and coax and mourn.
  'Suno, drink milk.'
  'Suno, study.'
  'Suno, take the exam.'
  And when they tired of being so patient with me and I still would not get up, they began to crackle and spit and storm. (p. 31)

As milk, an indulgence for the eldest son, recurs throughout the story and is always associated with the family's attempts to force Sunno to study for exams it becomes a symbol of parental expectations. It is a symbol that comes up repeatedly in the narrative and is therefore a motif.

- *An* example *from a text in your course:*

# Myth

Myths are stories that express the beliefs of a particular culture and tend to focus on how something came into being and contain supernatural characters.

- Classical myths include characters such as Aphrodite, Prometheus, Orpheus, and Zeus. References to mythology are common in literature. Helios was the Sun god in Greek Mythology and the subject of the ancient Colossus of Rhodes referred to in Sylvia Plath's poem 'The Colossus' (1998). Knowledge of this mythology and its historical significance allows the reader to access these associations to help in the interpretation and appreciation of the poem.

- *An* example *from a text in your course:*

---

## Narrator

---

Narrator is the voice that a writer uses to deliver the narrative, or story.

- Jonathan Swift's satirical essay 'A Modest Proposal' (1995; originally published in 1729) is a clear example of the distinction between the author and voice that the author creates through the use of a narrator. In this essay the narrator remarks, 'that a young healthy child well nursed is at a year old a most delicious, nourishing, and wholesome food, whether stewed, roasted, baked, or boiled,' in a disturbing satirical argument related to solving the economic problems of Ireland by eating the children of the poor. The cold, clinical tone of the narrator towards Ireland, mimicking the economic rationalism of the English Government of the time that Swift set out to satirize, is certainly not the voice of the author. The author creates a 'voice' through the narrator.

- *An* example *from a text in your course:*

---

## Occasion

---

Occasion is a particular event that part of the action of a narrative is structured around.

- 'Games at Twilight' (1998), a short story by Anita Desai is structured around an event, a game of hide-and-seek. This occasion supports the narrative as the reader is familiar with the rules and the motivations of the children involved in this particular game.

- *An* example *from a text in your course:*

# Onomatopoeia

Onomatopoeia refers to the use of a word whose pronunciation resembles the sound that the word describes. It can also refer to sounds which suggest a meaning.

- Two lines from Lord Tennyson's 'Come Down, O Maid, from yonder mountain height' from the poem 'The Princess' (2007) originally published in 1847 contain an interesting example of onomatopoeia:

    *The <u>moan</u> of doves in immemorial elms,*

    *And <u>murmuring</u> of innumerable bees.*

The word 'moan' not only resembles the soft noises that the doves make in the elms but suggests the sadness of separation. The word 'murmuring' likewise not only resembles the sound of the large group of bees that it describes but suggests agitation or latent power.

- *An example from a text in your course:*

# Paradox

Paradox is a statement that on the surface seems self contradictory but contains a truth that reconciles the contradiction.

- In George Orwell's novel *1984* (2003; originally published 1949) one of three paradoxical statements forming a slogan of the totalitarian regime governing the depicted society is 'War is Peace'. On the surface this statement is contradictory although as part of the rising action Winston, the protagonist learns that the Party, the governing body, maintains a constant state of war with their neighbors in order to maintain domestic control. Perpetual war means that the lower classes focus hate outwards and not at the party, shortages of produce and lives of drudgery are justified by the war efforts and the Party's rule is never actually threatened as war remains a series of border conflicts and shifting alliances. Therefore on closer inspection the seemingly contradictory statement 'War is Peace' contains a truth that reconciles the contradiction – for the Party, perpetual war on the borders does maintain a state of domestic peace.

- *An example from a text in your course:*

---

## Parody

---

Parody is the exaggerated and imitative use of another work's literary features to ridicule that work.

- Jonathon Swift's novel *Gulliver's Travels* (2003; originally published in 1726), through the use of Gulliver's exaggerated enthusiasm for the Laputan's discoveries, parodies the Royal Society of the time. The type of technical language used by the Laputan's was part of Swift's imitative use of the language of the Royal Society's papers.

- *An example from a text in your course:*

---

## Persona (voice)

---

Persona is the 'person' who speaks in a text such as the narrator in a novel or the speaker in a poem. The persona is often referred to as the voice. Although the persona/voice may convey the author's thoughts or views it is important to remember that the persona is not the author, the persona/voice is a construct of the author. It is useful to consider the *persona* as the origin of the *voice*. The attitude of the persona is *tone*.

- In the short story by Gabriel Garcia Marquez, 'I only came to use the phone' (Marquez, 1994; originally published in Spanish in 1992) the persona is constructed through the third person narration and the 'voice' is detached, displaying no surprise at the unusual turn of events that led Marie, the protagonist, to be accidentally committed to a mental asylum. The 'voice' does however display a sympathetic tone for Marie in terms of the narration of her abandonment by her boyfriend.

- *An example from a text in your course:*

# Personification

Personification is the embodiment of human qualities in inanimate objects.
- In Toni Morrison's novel *Beloved* (1987) an inanimate house takes on some disturbing human behaviors: 'Each fled at once – the moment the house committed what was for him the one insult not to be borne or witnessed a second time.'
- In Albert Camus' novel *The Stranger* (1989; originally published in French in 1942) cymbals of sunlight crashed on the protagonist's forehead while a scorching blade slashed at his eyelids and stabbed at his stinging eyes. This was apparently not a great day at the beach.
- *An example from a text in your course:*

# Plot

Plot is the series of events in a narrative.
- In the short story, 'The Saint' in *Strange Pilgrims* (1994; originally published in Spanish in 1992) by Gabriel García Márquez a chance meeting between two old friends sparks a recollection of events from their shared past. One of the friends, the narrator, tells the story of a Margarito Duarte whose seven year old daughter died at the age of seven but when, due to the construction of a dam, the coffin was moved it was found that the girl's body was still in tact, preserved perfectly, had no weight and smelt of the roses that she had been buried with; a miracle in Margarito's eyes. The narrative traces Margarito's journey from his village high in the Columbian Andes to Rome, carrying his daughter's weightless body in a small coffin, in order to appeal to the Vatican for her canonization. The story relates details of Margarito's time in Rome including his acquaintance with the narrator. The narrative ends with the narrator explaining the length of the father's wait and his suggestion that it was the father who was, in fact, the saint.

*This is a brief description of the series of events in the narrative although these events are only important for a literary analysis in terms of the significance that they have for the text as a whole as plot is only one literary feature, albeit an extremely important one.*

• *An* example *from a text in your course:*

---

## Point of View

---

Point of view is the perspective from which the narrative is delivered and is generally classified as a first person perspective, a second person perspective which is very rare, a third person (limited) perspective or a third person (omniscient) perspective.

• The point of view of *Silas Marner* by George Eliot (1994; originally published in 1861) is the third person (omniscient) perspective. The novel opens with the lines:

> In the days when the spinning-wheels hummed busily in the farmhouses – and even great ladies, clothed in silk and thread-lace, had their toy spinning-wheels of polished oak – there might be seen in districts far away among the lanes, or deep in the bosom of the hills, certain pallid undersized men, who, by the side of the brawny country folk, looked like the remnants of a disinherited race. (p. 9)

The omniscient, or all seeing, narrator is familiar with all aspects of this time period. The narrator is also familiar with what each of the characters think and feel, 'It was partly to this vague fear that Marner was indebted for protecting him from the persecution that his singularities might have drawn upon him…' (p. 13)

• *An* example *from a text in your course:*

---

## Protagonist

---

Protagonist is the main character in a narrative. The protagonist is not necessarily a 'good' character.

• Meursault is the protagonist in Albert Camus *The Stranger* (1989; originally published in French in 1942), a single main character whereas Emily Bronte's *Wuthering Heights* (2002; originally published in 1847) has two protagonists, Catherine and Heathcliff.

- *An* example *from a text in your course:*

---
## Repetition
---

Repetition is the repeated use any feature of a work such as a particular word, sound or image and is generally used for emphasis.

- In Shakespeare's play *Macbeth* 'blood' is an important motif symbolizing the guilt of both Macbeth and Lady Macbeth and repeated references are made to blood throughout the play. Repetition places emphasis on the repeated feature. The audience will hear Macbeth say this word 'blood' four times in less than twenty lines of dialogue with Lady Macbeth on stage. :

*Macbeth:*  It will have **blood**, they say; **blood** will have **blood**.   (3:4:151)

*Macbeth:*  All causes shall give way. I am in **blood**
Stepped so far that, should I wade no more,
Returning were as tedious as go'er.   (3:4:170)

- *An* example *from a text in your course:*

---
## Rhyme
---

Rhyme is the pattern that forms through the duplication of sounds.

- William Wordsworth's poem 'I Wandered Lonely as a Cloud' (2006), originally published in 1804, demonstrates a rhyme scheme of *ababcc*.

I wandered lonely as a *cloud*
That floats on high o'er vales and *hills*,
When all at once I saw a *crowd*,
A host, of golden *daffodils*;
Beside the lake, beneath the *trees*,
Fluttering and dancing in the *breeze*.

- *An example from a text in your course:*

---

# Satire

---

Satire is the use of ridicule to protest a particular folly or vice in society.

- In Wild's *The Importance of Being Earnest* (2005; originally published 1895) the arbitrary nature of idealism in society is ridiculed through Gwendolen's insistence on loving a man, any man, with the name Ernest without consideration of any other quality. Furthermore there is a clear suggestion that the popularity of idealism is due to commercial publications and that these magazines, viewed by the fashionable upper classes, are driving the content of religious sermons. The audience is left with the idea that Gwendolen has merely seized on the popular idea of having an 'ideal' and has made a superficial and arbitrary decision as to what her own ideal is going to be which appears to the audience as pure folly, especially as the plot revolves around a man using a fictitious name and living a double life - Ernest's real name, as far as he knows, is actually Jack.

    *Gwendolen:* We live as I hope you know, Mr Worthing, in an age of ideals. The fact that is mentioned in the more expensive monthly magazines, and has reached the provincial pulpits, I am told; and my ideal has always been to love some one of the name Ernest. There is something in that name that inspires complete confidence. The moment Algernon first mentioned to me that he had a friend called Ernest. I knew I was destined to love you.

- *An example from a text in your course:*

---

# Setting

---

Setting is the environment in which the action of the narrative occurs. The environment includes physical details of the place and circumstances as well as the time period. The environment also includes cultural, historical and socio-economic factors.

- David Williamson's play *Traveling North* (Williamson, 1993; originally published in 1979) set in Australia in various locations; Melbourne, North Queensland, Sydney and near Tweed Heads on the border of Queensland and New South Wales. The physical locations, warm and tropical North Queensland, damp and cold Melbourne and borderline Tweed Heads are important elements in the play. The play is set between 1969 and 1972 when commonly accepted roles in family were being increasingly challenged and this is also an important element of Williamson's play.

- *An example from a text in your course:*

## Simile

Simile is a comparison between objects or ideas. In a simile certain characteristics of one object or idea are transferred to the other generally using the words 'as' or 'like'. It is important to remember that the target idea or object retains its own identity in a simile which is the major difference between simile and metaphor.

- Albert Camus uses the following simile in *The Stranger* (1989; originally published in French in 1942) to express the violent nature of the experience of the protagonist: 'The light shot off the steel and it was like a long flashing blade cutting at my forehead.'

- *An example from a text in your course:*

## Soliloquy

Soliloquy in drama is a monologue where an actor appears to be thinking out loud. The soliloquy differs from an *aside* where an actor makes a brief remark directly to the audience.

- In Shakespeare's play *Othello* (2004; originally published approximately 1621) Iago delivers a powerful soliloquy at the end of Act 1 outlining his plan that seems to formulate as he speaks.

*Iago:*        *The Moor is of a free and open nature*
              *That thinks men honest that but seem to be so,*
              *And will as tenderly be led by the nose*
              *As asses are.*
              *I have't. It is engendered. Hell and night*
              *Must bring this monstrous birth to the world's light.*        *(1:3:447)*

- *An* example *from a text in your course:*

---

# Sound

---

Sound as a literary feature includes the use of rhyme, onomatopoeia, assonance, alliteration and auditory imagery. Although sound is an important aspect of drama it is also an important aspect of written texts in this sense.

- In Conrad's *Heart of Darkness* (2002; originally published in 1899) the protagonist Marlow comments that,

   'The voice of the surf heard now and then was a positive pleasure, like the voice of a brother. It was something natural, that had its reason, that had a meaning.' (p. 21) This auditory imagery of the surf is used to demonstrate Marlow's initial connection with the African continent as apposed to his lack of understanding of, or connection with, the colonial exploits that he described prior to hearing the sound of the surf as a, 'sordid farce acted in font of a sinister backcloth.' Later Marlow identifies with the sound of the drums as he journeys up the river into the heart of the continent in the same way that he identified with the sound of the surf. Remember; do not forget the importance of sound, even in a written text.

- *An* example *from a text in your course:*

---

# Speaker

---

Speaker can refer to either a character who is involved in dialogue or a monologue or it can refer to the narrator, the voice that a writer uses to deliver the narrative. This distinction is important when *tone* is considered as this term describes the attitude of the speaker to the audience. A character can adopt a particular tone towards another character and the narrator can adopt a particular tone toward the reader or audience. Generally tone is used in literary analysis in association with the latter, the attitude of the *speaker/narrator* to the reader or audience.

- The speaker in Camus' *The Stranger* is the protagonist Meursault, the story narrated from the first person perspective. The tone of Meursault, the speaker, is detached and unemotional relating events with a minimum of personal judgment evident.

- *An example from a text in your course:*

---
# Structure
---

Structure refers to how a text fits together, especially in reference to how parts of a text relate to each other. Usually this will relate to mechanical divisions such as chapters, acts or scenes. It may also refer to logical divisions such as rising action and falling action for example. Structure is related to form, the overall design of a text, which is often associated with genre types.

- Shakespeare structured his play's using five acts, each act a mechanical division serving a specific purpose.

- *An example from a text in your course:*

---
# Style
---

Style refers to the patterns that emerge from the choices an author makes in relation to literary features.

- If you had read Conrad's *Heart of Darkness* and then without knowing who the author was you started reading *Lord Jim* you may be able to guess that the author was the same person because there are some patterns in the choices that Conrad makes in relation to literary features which distinguish his work. You would recognize Conrad's style in this case as you would notice that in both texts:
  - relatively long and complex sentences are used (a pattern in the choice of syntax)
  - the use of language is very descriptive (a pattern in the choice of diction and imagery)
  - he uses technical vocabulary related to ships and life at sea (a pattern in the choice of diction)
  - the narrative is structured around an adventure involving journeys by sea and river (a pattern in the choice of plot)
  - the protagonist is a European male in a colonial setting, is portrayed as introspective, sympathizes more with the colonized than the colonizers and grows in understanding through the course of the narrative (a pattern in the choice of setting and characterization)

- *An* example *from a text in your course:*

# Subplot

Subplot is a minor sequence of events in a narrative.

- In Emily Bronte's *Wuthering Heights* (2002; originally published in 1847) a subplot of the main narrative is the marriage of Hindley to Frances, the birth of their son Hareton and the subsequent death of Frances. This subplot serves multiple purposes, supporting the main narrative. For example Frances's death reinforces the inhospitable and unforgiving atmosphere of Wuthering Heights. Also the birth of Hareton allows the reader to see Heathcliff save the life of the baby, Hareton, who is dropped while Hindley is drunk. Heathcliff instinctively catches the falling baby, saving his life and although Heathcliff instantly regrets his actions, this scene provides further ambiguity to Healthcliff's true nature and by saving the life of a defenseless and motherless Hareton the reader is able to build sympathy for the character, Heathcliff, despite his hatred for the baby. By identifying a series of events as a subplot you are able to discuss the significance of this part to the whole and this is particularly useful in a text with a complex narrative structure.

- *An* example *from a text in your course:*

# Subtext

Subtext refers to the underlying meaning of a statement or series of events, what is not said or done but what the reader or audience interprets.

- In George Orwell's *Animal Farm* (1990; originally published in 1945) the character Squealer can be interpreted as a representation of the use of the Russian media by Stalin. This association is not explicitly stated and is therefore defined as a subtext.

- *An* example *from a text in your course:*

# Symbol

A symbol is an, person, place or other relatively concrete object or action which stands for an abstract idea. There is always an aspect of the literal definition which connects to the figurative meaning

- 'Sleep' literally means the body's *rest* cycle. In the play *Macbeth* (2004; originally published in approximately 1603) by Shakespeare sleep takes on the additional figurative meaning of 'peace' as both Macbeth and Lady Macbeth are deprived of sleep – and therefore deprived of 'peace' through this use of symbolism, after their murder of Duncan.

- 'Curtain' literally means material that hangs in a window as a *screen*. In the play *Thunderstorm* (2001; originally published in Chinese in 1933) by Tsao Yu the 'closing of the curtains' take on the additional figurative meaning of 'moral corruption and isolation'. The patriarch of the household Zhou Puyuan constantly closes the curtains in his house so outsiders cannot see inside with the consequence that the family is no longer able to see the outside world.

- *An* example *from a text in your course:*

# Syntax (sentence structure)

Syntax is the structure of a sentence.

- In Albert Camus' *The Stranger* (1989; originally published in French in 1942) the sentences are short and simple reflecting the perspective on life of the protagonist, Meursault. In Joseph Conrad's *Heart of Darkness* (2002; originally published in 1899) the sentences are long and complex creating intense visual imagery.

- *An* example *from a text in your course:*

---

# Theme

---

Theme is an idea that pervades a text. Themes are statements that inform the reader about how the world is.

- In *Games at Twilight* (1998) the short story 'Games at Twilight' by Anita Desai, the idea that a child's realization of their own place in the real world is a painful and inevitable experience is presented. This theme is a statement not limited to the events of the narrative but is both timeless and universal.

- *An* example *from a text in your course:*

---

# Tone

---

Tone is the attitude of the speaker (usually the narrator) to the reader or audience. It can also refer to the attitude of one character to another within a narrative.

- In George Orwell's *1984* (2003; originally published 1949) in Room 101 O'Brien adopts a cold, clinical tone towards Winston reflecting the imbalance in their power relationship as well as the lack of human warmth in the totalitarian Party. (character to character)

- In Jonathan Swift's 'A Modest Proposal' (1995; originally published in 1729) the narrator adopts a cold, clinical tone towards the reader, satirizing the lack of feeling in the perspective of economic rationalism. (narrator to reader/audience)

- Some words commonly used to describe tone, as well as the atmosphere/mood that the tone helps to create.

- *An* example *from a text in your course:*

## Your tools for literary analysis

Remember that all of these words allow you to analyze a text; to take it apart, to see how each part works as a component of a larger whole as well as to see how each component part supports the others.

# Examples of Completed Activities

In this section you will find examples of the activities used in this booklet. These are intended as ideas to help you complete each of the activities and provide examples of the types of spoken or written language that each activity supports.

*Activity 1: Considering Context*

## Activity 1: Considering Context

**Assessment Criteria:** meaningful and perceptive linking of works / thorough knowledge and understanding of the content of the extract or works

**Description:** Before you start the course you already have a bank of knowledge that will help you to understand the texts. There may also be some misunderstandings that need clearing up.

1. Write down notes regarding what you know about the text, author, time period, language or geographic region.

2. In pairs share your own information and include new pieces of information from your partner in your workbook.

3. During the course when you begin to look at a text as a class bring all your ideas together on the board to both share ideas and dispel misunderstandings.

# Text 1

| | |
|---|---|
| **Title:** | *Heart of Darkness* |
| **Author:** | **Joseph Conrad** |
| **Dates:** | Originally published in 1899 |

**Country and language of original publication:**
England – published in English

## What do you know about this text, author, time period, language, geographic region or political situation that may be relevant?

- Joseph Conrad was fascinated by the sea. He wrote *Lord Jim* which was also linked to sea voyages. Conrad was Polish and English was his second language.

- The movie *Apocalypse Now* is a modern adaptation of the ideas in this novel situated in the Vietnam War.

- Belgium, or at least Belgian's King Leopold, was in the process of colonizing the area near the Congo River where Conrad situated the bulk of the narrative.

- Conrad questioned the idea of the noble savage – primitive goodness uncorrupted by civilization - that had been popular, since Rousseau's publication of *Emile* in 1762. Conrad wondered at the horror of European colonization and the nature of the human heart, central themes in *Heart of Darkness*.

- In 1975 *Heart of Darkness* came under criticism from Nigerian novelist Chinua Achebe for being racist and the text was subsequently defended as being an expose on imperialist violence and racism.

*(Any general knowledge that you have about the text can go in here. You can check whether it is accurate with your teacher or peers or through further research. This is a time to validate existing knowledge, dispel misunderstandings and construct new knowledge. You will find a text more interesting when you know something about the context within which it was written.)*

*Activity 2: Quote Bank*

## Activity 2: Quote Bank

**Assessment Criteria:** detailed and persuasive references to the works
**Description:**

- Choose a direct reference from a character in your text. In the case of poetry choose a specific line.

- Comment on the relevance of the reference – what it tells us about the character / poem.

- Finally, comment on the links between these references in terms of their significance for the text as a whole.

**Text: Text:**   *Wuthering Heights* by Emily Bronte
**Character One:**   Heathcliff
**Quote / Reference 1:** Heathcliff's reception as narrated by Nelly to Mr. Lockwood

*He leant his two elbows on his knees, and his chin on his hands, and remained wrapt in dumb meditation. On my inquiring the subject of his meditation, he answered gravely –*
*"I'm trying to settle how I shall pay Hindley back. I don't care how long I wait, if I can only do it at last. I hope he will not die before I do!"*
*"For shame, Heathcliff!" said I. "It is for God to punish wicked people; we should learn to forgive."*
*"No, God won't have the satisfaction that I shall," he returned. "I only wish I knew the best way! Let me alone, and I'll plan it out: while I'm thinking of that I don't feel."*

**Significance:**
This quote helps to develop the reader's sympathy for Heathcliff as we can see that the revenge that is foreshadowed in this scene has its origin in the pain of a powerless and mistreated young boy. The incongruent image of a small boy taking over the responsibility for punishment from God is presented. This divine punishment generally associated with Judgment Day in a biblical sense, strengthens the metaphoric link between Heathcliff and the Devil, the other being who challenged God and was eventually punished for his actions.

**Quote / Reference 2:** Part of a conversation between Heathcliff and Catherine Linton narrated by Nelly to Mr. Lockwood
*'I seek no revenge on you,' replied Heathcliff less vehemently. 'That's not the plan. The tyrant grinds down his slaves and they don't turn against him; they crush those beneath them. You are welcome to torture me to death for your amusement, only allow me to amuse myself a little in the same style, and refrain from insults as much as you are able. Having leveled my palace, don't erect a hovel and complacently admire your own charity in giving me that for a home. If I imagined you really wished me to marry Isabella, I'd cut my throat!'*

**Significance:**

Heathcliff's conversation with Catherine Linton again displays the origin of Heathcliff's behavior in the mistreatment of Heathcliff by other characters – in this case Catherine herself. It allows the reader to witness the unfolding of Healthcliff's plan as to how he was going to pay Hindley back – the fact that this plan involves more people than just Hindley is clear. The reference to the tyrant alludes to Heathcliff's own treatment of others as well as to Catherine's treatment of Heathcliff. Healthcliff's brutal nature, lack of sympathy, amusement at the torment of others, sense of anger at past injustice as well as his devotion to Catherine and confidence in the reciprocal nature of their love is clear. Heathcliff's use of the hovel metaphor to describe the state of their relationship demonstrates to the reader how deeply Heathcliff has been hurt by Catherine's actions.

**Quote / Reference 3:** A section of a letter from Isabella to Nelly read by Nelly to Mr. Lockwood

*The remainder of my letter is for yourself alone. I want to ask you two questions; the first is – How did you contrive to preserve the common sympathies of human nature when you resided here? I cannot recognize any sentiment which those around share with me.*

*The second question, I have great interest in; it is this – Is Mr. Heathcliff a man? If so, is he mad? And if not, is he a devil? I shan't tell my reasons for making this inquiry; but I beseech you to explain, in you can, what I have married: that is, when you call to see me; and you must call, Ellen, very soon. Don't write but come, and bring me something from Edgar.*

**Significance:**

This quote suggests a link between the physical and natural environments. The contrast between the Grange and the Heights is presented in terms of its link to the social conditions existing in the respective locations. The reference to Healthcliff's unknown origins when Heathcliff came to the house is important here as Nelly would not actually be able to answer the second question. The seemingly detached tone that Isabella asks about Heathcliff's nature suggests horrific experience – a state of shock perhaps – and the reader is left wondering at the nature of Isabella's treatment.

Isabella has represented innocence and it is this destruction of innocence that is most apparent in her tone.

## Comment on the links between these quotes:

The association of Heathcliff with the devil is supported by all thee quotes combining the unknown origins with the inhuman enjoyment of inflicting suffering on an innocent.

There is something inhuman about Heathcliff's actions although when we view his actions in light of his treatment when he first came to the house as seen through Nelly's eyes the reader can sympathize at one level. The tyrant comment could be interpreted in relation to Catherine's treatment of him as he crushes the heart of Isabella in turn –'those under him'. Interestingly, the comment is not applicable to Hindley's treatment of Heathcliff as can be seen in the top quote where Heathcliff does 'turn against' him as the response is to plan revenge on the original tyrant who was in fact Hindley.

All of these quotes stood out to me because I found myself wondering what I would do in these situations if I were Heathcliff. I found that I admired him in a way for standing up to the brutality of Hindley and for the strength of his love for Catherine. I couldn't however admire anything about his treatment of Isabella, especially as she was an outsider to all of the previous action and was in effect an innocent bystander.

## Activity 3: Quote Builder

**Assessment Criteria:** ideas are convincing and show independence of thought
**Description:** Break into small groups or pairs. In turn each group or pair presents a short quote from the text to the opposing team.
The opposing team must supply three pieces of information after hearing the quote:

- Which character the quote is from
- The context in which it appeared in the text
- The significance of the quote for the overall text

The first two have definite answers although the last will be dependent on individual interpretations. All answers that can be justified are acceptable – the language used in the justification of the response is an important aspect of this activity.

## Quote Builder: Round 1 Notes

**Our Quote** (Write it here so you can read it out to the opposition)
'But German sounds a thoroughly respectable language, and indeed, I believe it is so.'

**Character:**
Lady Bracknell from *The Importance of Being Ernest* by Oscar Wilde

**Context:**
Lady Bracknell says this to Algernon at his flat just before they leave Jack and Gwendolen alone together.

**Significance:**
This is part of a string of epigrams that come through the speech of Lady Bracknell which satirize the shallowness and arbitrary nature of the judgments that are passed on respectability. The idea that a system of language governs respectability as apposed to the content of an utterance has an element of irony considering that the play itself is presented in a respectable language according to Lady Bracknell, English, but the ideas presented satirize the belief systems and institutions of Victorian society - hardly a respectable use of this respectable language.

*Another possible approach could be:*

This quote demonstrates how the awarding of respectability is controlled by the upper class of society and that they award respectability in very arbitrary and senseless ways. Because of the other absurd things that Lady Bracknell is portrayed as saying in the play the audience will be easily able to recognize the absurdity of the remark.

*(These are just two examples of possible responses. Different responses will be applied to the same quotes and it is important to recognize the role of interpretation in a response to a text. The important point is to be able to justify an interpretation and use appropriate literary terminology.)*

## Activity 4: Literary Feature Analysis

**Assessment Criteria:** *critical analysis of the effects of the literary features of the works consistently well illustrated by persuasive examples*

**Description:**

- Copy a passage from your text into one of the spaces below.

- Identify a literary feature and comment on this feature in the 'Literary features' table.

### Leo Tolstoy: *Anna Karenina* (Extract)
Copy or paste a short passage from your text here

Seryozha's eyes, which had been shining with affection and joy, lost their brilliance under his father's gaze. It was the same long familiar tone in which his father always addressed him and to which Seryozha had already learned how to adapt himself. His father always talked to him, so Seryozha felt, as though he were addressing some imaginary boy out of a book who was quite unlike Seryozha. And when he was with his father Seryozha always tried to be that imaginary boy out of a book.

"You understand that, I hope?" said his father.

"Yes, sir," replied Seryozha, pretending to be that imaginary boy.

(Tolstoy, *Anna Karenina*, 1961; originally published in Russian in 1877)

Is this not one of the saddest things that you have ever read!

### Literary Feature 1:
- **Describe a literary feature that you can see in the passage above.**

A motif of 'role play' can be recognized in this passage. This idea of people pretending to be someone that they are not recurs throughout the novel.

- **Provide specific examples from the text.**

The idea of pretence is evident is Seryozha's reply to his father when he pretends to be the imaginary boy that his father is addressing. As Seryozha has adapted himself to this pretence and as it is stated that his father always uses this tone, the reader can recognize that this is a long standing pattern in their relationship.

- **Describe the effect this literary feature has on the reader/audience.**

The use of this motif to illustrate the estrangement of father and son engenders a feeling of sympathy for Seryozha as well as for Karenina, his father. This sympathy is also generated through the use of the image of Seryozha's eyes loosing the brilliance of their affection and joy, a direct affect of the role play. This scene foreshadows an older Seryozha who is doomed to repeat the father's mistakes. This estrangement between father and son represents the general effect of role play in society.

- **Outline links of this literary feature to others.**

The reader, through the use of this motif within Karenina's home life can see a parallel between Karenina's relationship with his son and his relationship with the Russian Court where Karenina is constantly role playing. By illustrating Seryozha's growing awareness of this need to play roles the reader recognizes the inevitability of the son making the same mistakes as his father.

If you want to see what all of this looks like when you put it together just write it out into a paragraph.

> A motif of 'role play' can be recognized in this passage. This idea of people pretending to be someone that they are not recurs throughout the novel. The idea of pretence is evident is Seryozha's reply to his father when he pretends to be the imaginary boy that his father is addressing. As Seryozha has adapted himself to this pretence and it is stated that his father always uses this tone the reader can recognize that this is a long standing pattern in their relationship. The use of this motif to illustrate the estrangement of father and son engenders a feeling of sympathy for Seryozha as well as Karenina, his father. This sympathy is also generated through the use of the image of Seryozha's eyes loosing the brilliance of their affection and joy, a direct affect of the role play and foreshadows an older Seryozha who is doomed to repeat the father's mistakes. The reader, through the use of this motif within Karenina's home life can see a parallel between Karenina's relationship with his son and his relationship with the Russian Court where Karenina is constantly role playing. By illustrating Seryozha's growing awareness of this need to play roles the reader recognizes the inevitability of the son making the same mistakes as his father.

As the persuasiveness of your responses will ultimately depend on the level of detail that you are able to provide, add as much relevant detail into each section as possible. As these sections are all eventually joined together, paying attention to the level of detail in these individual sections will provide you with material to make a very detailed and persuasive response overall.

## Activity 4: Shared Reading Response

**Assessment Criteria:** meaningful and perceptive linking of works
**Description:**

- In small groups students take turns speaking about the last thing that you read - generally the current work.

- The listener is required to ask questions as they go along using the following prompt.

- Both the listener and the speaker need to make note of any questions asked at the end of the activity

**Prompt to assist with questioning**

# As the listener you are required to ask questions related to any of the following:

- **The speaker's knowledge of the content**

- **How parts of the work relate to the work as a whole and to other works?**

- **What effects literary features have on the reader's response?**

*As a listener you need to help the speaker stay focused and to support their ideas with specific references from the work. Your questioning can help them to do this. The speaker needs to use accurate, clear and precise language. By seeking clarification of points you can help the speaker to do this.*

**Shared Reading Response: Record Sheet for questions asked and responses**

## The speaker's knowledge of the content

Why couldn't Macbeth kill Duncan by himself? *Macbeth* (Shakespeare, 2004; originally published in approximately 1603)

How did Ravi feel when he was hiding in the shed? 'Games at Twilight' (Desai, 1998)

Why did Francis's daughters dislike Frank? *Travelling North* (Willianson, Travelling North, 1993; originally published in 1979)

What was the relationship between Crofts and Mrs Warren? *Mrs Warren's Profession* (Shaw, 1991; originally published in 1902)

What significance did the idea of work hold for Irena at the beginning of the play? *Three Sisters* (Chekhov, 1990; originally published in Russian in 1901)

*Questions for different texts are asked here although in your Workbook they will generally all be related to the one targeted text. Try to ask questions that pick up on ideas that have been mentioned to push the speaker into greater detail. For example the first question is one that you could ask if the speaker mentioned that Lady Macbeth assisted in the murder of Duncan.*

## How parts of the work relate to the work as a whole and to other works?

Does Plath (1998) use any other images from famous artistic work to illustrate her poems as she has done in 'Two Views of a Cadaver Room' with the Flemish lovers?

What is the significance of 'milk' in the short stories told by Desai in *Games at Twilight* (1998)?

How does Irena's wistful tone at the start of the play compare to her tone in the final Act of *Three Sisters* (Chekhov, 1990; originally published in Russian in 1901)?

In *Heart of Darkness* did Marlow achieve what he intended to do when he set out (Conrad, 2002; originally published in 1899)?

What was Frances's motivation for wanting to keep heading north throughout the play in *Travelling North* (Willianson, Travelling North, 1993; originally published in 1979)?

# What effects literary features have on the reader's response?

How was Suno's perception of the atmosphere of the park in 'Studies in the Park' altered by his experience with the dying figure in black on the bench? (Desai, 1998)

Why didn't *Macbeth* start on a bright, sunny day (Shakespeare, 2004; originally published in approximately 1603)?

What role did cigarettes play as a motif in *Anna Karenina* (Tolstoy, 1961; originally published in Russian in 1877)?

How did the Samurai in Endo Shusaku's *The Samurai* (1982; originally published in Japanese in 1980) compare as a character to Mitsuko in *Deep River* (Endo, 1994; originally published in Japanese in 1993)? Who do you think was the more honest of the two characters?

How do the subjects in Marquez's *Strange Pilgrims* (Marquez, 1994; originally published in Spanish in 1992) compare to those in Desai's *Games at Twilight* (Desai, 1998) Which of the short stories contained images related most closely to your own life experiences?

*Again, try to pick up a thread from something that the speaker has mentioned and follow up to push for more detail of the literary features. For example, if the speaker mentioned Suno's growing preference for the atmosphere of the park you could ask a question linking the image of the dying women with this atmosphere.*

## Other questions

What have you found to be the most difficult part of understanding the ideas in these texts?

What would you have done if you were Winston when the rats were coming? (Orwell, 1984, 2003; originally published 1949)

*(Anything you like can go in here - anything that you happen to be wondering about.)*

## Activities 6 & 7: Connecting Theme and Literary Features in a Text

**Assessment Criteria:** in-depth knowledge of, and very good insight into, aspects of the work / purposeful and effective structure / supporting examples are well integrated

**Description:**

- Identify an idea, or theme, expressed through the text you are analyzing.

- Select up to three literary features that appear in the work that in some way support or are related to that identified idea or theme. Highlight these literary features from the given list. Definitions appear in the Vocabulary Log.

- Explain how the chosen literary features support this idea, or theme in the sections below.

- When completing the sections you should attempt to make links between the literary features in terms of how they support each other in the text.

### George Orwell: *Animal Farm* (Extract)

A few days later, when the terror caused by the executions had died down, some of the animals remembered-or thought they remembered-that the Sixth Commandment decreed "No animal shall kill any other animal." And though no one cared to mention it in the hearing of the pigs or the dogs, it was felt that the killings which had taken place did not square with this. Clover asked Benjamin to read her the Sixth Commandment, and when Benjamin, as usual, said that he refused to meddle in such matters, she fetched Muriel. Muriel read the Commandment for her. It ran: "No animal shall kill any other animal without cause." Somehow or other, the last two words had slipped out of the animals' memory. But they saw now that the Commandment had not been violated; for clearly there was good reason for killing the traitors who had leagued themselves with Snowball.

Throughout the year the animals worked even harder than they had worked in the previous year to rebuild the windmill, with walls twice as thick as before, and to finish it by the appointed date, together with the regular work of the farm, was a tremendous labour. There were times when it seemed to the animals that they worked longer hours and fed no better than they had done in Jones's day. On Sunday mornings Squealer, holding down a long strip of paper with his trotter, would read out to them lists of figures proving that the production of every class of foodstuff had increased by two hundred per cent, three hundred per cent, or five hundred per cent, as the case might be. The animals saw no reason to disbelieve him, especially as they could no longer remember very clearly what conditions had been like before the Rebellion. All the same, there were days when they felt that they would sooner have had less figures and more food.

All orders were now issued through Squealer or one of the other pigs. Napoleon himself was not seen in public as often as once in a fortnight. When he did appear, he was attended not only by his retinue of dogs but by a black cockerel who marched in front of him and acted as a kind of trumpeter, letting out a loud "cock-a-doodle-doo" before Napoleon spoke. Even in the farmhouse, it was said, Napoleon inhabited separate apartments from the others. He took his meals alone, with two dogs to wait upon him, and always ate from the Crown Derby dinner service which had been in the glass cupboard in the drawing-room. It was also announced that the gun would be fired every year on Napoleon's birthday, as well as on the other two anniversaries.

Napoleon was now never spoken of simply as "Napoleon." He was always referred to in formal style as "our Leader, Comrade Napoleon," and this pigs liked to invent for him such titles as Father of All Animals, Terror of Mankind, Protector of the Sheep-fold, Ducklings' Friend, and the like. In his speeches, Squealer would talk with the tears rolling down his cheeks of Napoleon's wisdom the goodness of his heart, and the deep love he bore to all animals everywhere, even and especially the unhappy animals who still lived in ignorance and slavery on other farms. It had become usual to give Napoleon the credit for every successful achievement and every stroke of good fortune. You would often hear one hen remark to another, "Under the guidance of our Leader, Comrade Napoleon, I have laid five eggs in six days"; or two cows, enjoying a drink at the pool, would exclaim, "Thanks to the leadership of Comrade Napoleon, how excellent this water tastes!"

*(Orwell, 1990; originally published in 1945)*

*In the following exercise three literary features will be examined. One has been chosen which will be treated as the 'aspect' of the discussion- the most important literary feature. This is merely a choice that I have made in order to structure the discussion so that I am able to explain how literary features work together. As you will see I merely introduce diction and then discuss how the other three features support this literary feature in relation to the theme. You should be trying to show that you are aware of how the literary features support each other. You can practice this while you take your notes in the Workbook. Good Luck!*

---

## Text: *Animal Farm*

---

**Theme/Ideas expressed through a text:** The exercise of power through the control of language

**Literary features identified:**

Allegory, Alliteration, Allusion, Antagonist, Aside, Association, Assonance, Atmosphere, Audience, Blank Verse, Caesura, Caricature, **Characterization,** Climax, Connotation, Denotation, Denouement, Dialogue, **Diction,** Enjambment, Euphemism, Flashback, Foreshadowing, Form, Framed Narrative, Free Verse, Genre, Hyperbole, Imagery, **Irony**, **Metaphor**, Meter, Metonymy, Mood, Motif, Myth, Narrator, Occasion, Onomatopoeia, Paradox, Parody, Persona, Personification, Plot, Point of View, Protagonist, Repetition, Rhyme, Satire, Setting, Simile, Soliloquy, Sound, Speaker, Structure, Style, Subplot, Subtext, Symbol, Syntax (sentence structure), Theme, Tone

---

### Literary Feature 1: Diction

---

**Describe a literary feature that you can identify in your text.**

Diction, in terms of the use of concrete nouns, has a clear effect on the text.

**Provide specific examples from the text.**

Concrete nouns: pigs, dogs, Commandment (repeatedly) animal, execution

**Describe the effect this literary feature has on the reader/audience.**

Nouns tend to be more concrete when the pigs are speaking. The concrete nouns reflect the concrete world that the animals live in. In this passage the animals' reasoning regarding the execution was based primarily on the Commandments; concrete objects. The absence of any abstract nouns (right / wrong / justice / compassion etc) demonstrated this deficiency in their reasoning from a human perspective. The pigs were constantly able to manipulate the other animals through the control of concrete elements such as the Commandments. Abstract concepts represented by words such as freedom were only used by the pigs. The reader can sense the power exerted by the pigs over the other animals in the control of these concepts through their language use.

**Outline links of this literary feature to other literary features.**

This use diction is supported by characterization as the types of words used by specific characters help to define their membership to different groups in the political landscape of the farm.

## Literary Feature 2: Characterization

### Describe a literary feature that you can identify in your text.

Characterization: Each character in the novel represents a group. Squealer for example, is a pig representing those who use language to manipulate information in order to consolidate political power.

### Provide specific examples from the text.

We see Squealer lying to the other animals about rising food production in this passage and he is able to manipulate the truth through language as the animals remember less and less about conditions before. This is one of many pieces of propaganda offered to the animals throughout the novel.

### Describe the effect this literary feature has on the reader/audience.

Squealer's use of language represents to the reader the dangers of propaganda and its insidious power to influence social norms. The language use of Squealer allows the reader to appreciate the danger of having unquestioned, arbitrary rules that can be changed without explanation by the ruling party. The Pigs do this with the Commandments.

### Outline links of this literary feature to other literary features.

The Commandments, the ultimate tool of language control used by the pigs, have strong metaphoric associations which help to create a sense of dramatic irony as the narrative progresses.

## Literary Feature 3: Metaphor

### Describe a literary feature that you can identify in your text.

Metaphor: The Commandments with their strong metaphoric associations to religious dogma provide a physical place for language, controlled by the pigs, to be set in stone – literally.

### Provide specific examples from the text.

'Muriel read the Commandment for her. It ran: "No animal shall kill any other animal without cause." Somehow or other, the last two words had slipped out of the animals' memory.' These physical Commandments were powerful enough to override the animals' memories.

### Describe the effect this literary feature has on the reader/audience.

A form of dramatic irony is established where the reader is aware of information that the characters in the novel are not, through the manipulation of language in the Commandments. '...some of the animals remembered-or thought they remembered...' The reader is aware of the manipulation and a sense of tension is created as the reader is powerless to intervene.

**Outline links of this literary feature to other literary features.**
The metaphoric association of the Commandments to religious dogma links to the use of diction, the control of word choice, and the power of language in the political landscape.

**It is a good idea to put your thoughts together in a few paragraphs:**

The exercise of power through the control of language is an important theme in *Animal Farm*. Orwell uses diction to portray this idea throughout the novel and characterization, metaphor and irony are also used to support this significant aspect of the novel.

The use of diction when presenting this theme is illustrated by Orwell's choice to use nouns that tend to be more concrete when the pigs are speaking. The concrete nouns reflect the concrete world that the animals live in. In this passage the animals' reasoning regarding the execution was based primarily on the Commandments; concrete objects. The use of concrete nouns such as 'pigs', 'dogs', 'Commandment', 'animal' and 'execution' contrast sharply with the absence of any abstract nouns such as 'right', 'wrong', 'justice' or 'compassion'. The absence of these abstract words demonstrates a deficiency in the animal's reasoning from a human perspective. The effect of this use of diction was evident as the pigs were constantly able to manipulate the other animals through the control of concrete elements such as the Commandments. Abstract concepts such as freedom were controlled by the pigs and used only to manipulate the animals. All arguments were justified through the concrete language of the Commandments.

Characterization supports this use of diction as each character uses different language which relates to the different groups in the political landscape represented on the farm. Each character in the novel represents a group such as squealer for example, a pig representing those who use language in order to manipulate information to consolidate political power. We see Squealer lying to the other animals about rising food production in this passage. Squealer is able to manipulate the truth through language as the animals remember less and less about conditions before.

The use of metaphor further supports the use of diction as the Commandments with their strong metaphoric associations to religious dogma provide a physical place for language, controlled by the pigs, to be set in stone – literally. These physical Commandments were powerful enough to override the animals' memories as can be seen in the following lines: *'Muriel read the Commandment for her. It ran: "No animal shall kill any other animal without cause." Somehow or other, the last two words had slipped out of the animals' memory.'*

Irony is also used to support the use of diction. A form of dramatic irony is established where the reader is aware of information that the characters are not through the manipulation of language in the Commandments as is evident in the lines, '…some of the animals remembered-or thought they remembered…', where the reader is aware of the manipulation. The use of irony here allows the reader to see the pigs' ability to exercise control over the other animals through their manipulation of the language of the farm.

*Many combinations of the literary features could have worked for this passage. Just choose ones that seem to fit easily. A brief introduction to your short piece of writing will allow the reader to follow your thought processes more easily and make sure that you use paragraphs with a topic sentence. This is not supposed to be a polished piece of writing. It is a place to practice making these connections while maintaining a logical coherence in your writing.*

## Activity 8: Analyzing Exam Questions

**Assessment Criteria:** logical coherence, concise use of language, response to demands of question

**Description:**

- Choose an examination question from the following list. Identify works to which the question will be addressed.

- Identify and highlight the major concepts in the question. These are the words that you think are the most important; the essence of the question.

- Take these words and add some qualifying information showing how these words connect to the chosen works.

- Use these groups of words in your introductory paragraph.

- The words should also appear consistently throughout the rest of your response.

*Remember that exam questions present you with a wide range of possible* **aspects** *that you could use as ideas to pursue in other types of assignments such as oral commentaries. Each exam question represents a possible approach to the literary analysis of a text. Over time this activity will provide you with a bank of ideas to use when analyzing literature independently.*

**The following steps illustrate the simple process:**

- Choose an examination question from the following list. Identify works to which the question will be addressed.

  - Question: How do guilt and/or blame contribute to conflict and the overall effect in a literary work?

  - Text: *1984* by George Orwell (You may need more than one text if the task specifies this.)

  -

- Identify and highlight the major concepts in the question. These are the words that you think are the most important; the essence of the question.

  - How do **guilt** and/or **blame** contribute to **conflict** and the overall effect in a literary work?
    1......**blame** and **guilt**................
    2......**conflict**..............................

- Take these words and add some qualifying information showing how these words connect to the chosen works.

- An idea that came to me when I read this question was that in *1984* the Party blamed Winston for his lack of love for Big Brother and required Winston to accept this blame and feel the associated guilt. Winston refused to do this. Eventually the Party forced him to feel this guilt and it was only then that Winston was able to love Big Brother. In this sense, an individual poses a threat to the state if he or she does not feel guilt for the things that the state blames them for. This is dangerous because if the individual does not feel guilt it shows that they do not accept the blame. What would happen if they **all** started blaming the state for their problems?

- From these initial thoughts came some qualifying information that can be added to the chosen words.

  1......'**blame** and **guilt** imposed by the state on individuals '...

  2......'**conflict** between the individual and the state'...

(The word qualifying is used here as it is not just any 'blame and guilt' but specifically the *blame and guilt imposed by the state on individuals*. It is also not just any conflict but specifically, the *conflict between the individual and the state*.)

- Use these groups of words in your introductory paragraph.
- The words should also appear consistently throughout the rest of your response.

**Sample introductory paragraph:**

**Blame** and **guilt** imposed by the state on individuals leads to **conflict** between the individual and the state as the decision of a person not to accept the **blame** for their own circumstances represents a clear threat to an authoritarian state. This idea is clearly illustrated in Orwell's *1984* through the **characterization** of Julia and Winston where acceptance and non-acceptance of **blame** are clearly contrasted. The contrasting **characterization** of Winston and Julia is supported by a range of **imagery** associated with curiosity and acceptance. Furthermore the clinical, investigative **tone** of O'Brien clearly mirror's the avid curiosity of Winston who continues to ask questions, refusing to accept the **blame** for his circumstances. This contrast demonstrates the nature of the power imbalance between the individual and the state, represented by the Party, as the reader eventually realizes the absurdity of Winston's individual hopes for freedom when his questions are finally answered. From this comparison it is clear that it is the Party's attention to the issue of **guilt** in the individual that ensures that they will always remain victorious in the **conflict** between the individual and the state as long as **blame** is accepted by the wider population. In this way, **blame** and **guilt** are the Party's most potent weapons; Winston's refusal to accept this **blame** and feel this **guilt** was the Party's greatest threat.

*(Use highlighters to see where the terms that you selected are used in the opening paragraph. You should see them referred to multiple times. You should also see at least a reference to specific literary features. Use a highlighter and see what patterns appear.)*